A LONG WAY GONE

Ishmael Beah

AUTHORED by Todd Gordon
UPDATED AND REVISED by Christine McKeever

COVER DESIGN by Table XI Partners LLC
COVER PHOTO by Olivia Verma and © 2005 GradeSaver, LLC

BOOK DESIGN by Table XI Partners LLC

Published by GradeSaver LLC, www.gradesaver.com

First published in the United States of America by GradeSaver LLC. 2012

ISBN 978-1-60259-304-6

Printed in the United States of America

For other products and additional information please visit http://www.gradesaver.com

Table of Contents

Table of Contents

Table of Contents

Biography of Beah, Ishmael (1980-)

Ishmael Beah was born in Sierra Leone in 1980. When he was 13, he was forced to become a child soldier during the civil war between the Sierra Leonean government and the Revolutionary United Front (RUF). For the next four years, Beah witnessed numerous atrocities and was forced to kill and torture people in the name of war.

He was rescued from the government army by The United Nations Children's Fund (UNICEF) and given a chance at a new life with his uncle. Beah was later chosen as one of two children to represent Sierra Leone at the United Nations First International Children's Parliament. His heartfelt account of the violence he faced and his testimony of the existence of thousands of children like him moved the UN. Laura Simms, a member of the UN, eventually adopted Beah as her son. In 1998, Beah moved to New York City with Simms. Beah is a graduate of the United Nations International School and Oberlin College.

Beah is a member of the Human Rights Watch Children's Rights Division Advisory Committee and has spoken to various governmental bodies about the plight of children affected by war. He is also the head of the Ishmael Beah Foundation, dedicated to helping former child soldiers find new lives by reintegrating into society. He currently lives in Brooklyn, New York.

About A Long Way Gone

According to New York Times book reviewer William Boyd, "The great benefit of Ishmael Beah's memoir, A Long Way Gone, is that it may help us arrive at an understanding of this situation. Beah's autobiography is almost unique, as far as I can determine -- perhaps the first time that a child soldier has been able to give literary voice to one of the most distressing phenomena of the late 20th century: the rise of the pubescent (or even prepubescent) warrior-killer."

A Long Way Gone is Ishmael Beah's memoir recounting his life in Sierra Leone just prior to and immediately after an attack by the Revolutionary United Front (RUF) soldiers on his home village. Beah moves through the vivid memories in a somewhat chronological order, often utilizing flashbacks in appropriate places for added poignancy. Once the book reaches its final chapters, it becomes clear to the reader that what Beah has done is to put into written form a more detailed version of the words he used to move the United Nations to action in Sierra Leone and its neighboring regions.

Beah attempts a journalistic, matter-of-fact tone throughout, most likely to accentuate how desensitized he had become to the horrors around him. He reports matters of maiming and death with simple, direct statements. Ultimately, it is up to the reader to judge the atrocity of both the act and its apparent lack of impact on the perpetrator(s). Conversely, Beah gives over to mellifluous descriptions of natural beauty and nostalgic reminiscences of family occasions to provide a counterpoint to the violence and inhumanity he experiences as both perpetrator and victim.

A Long Way Gone is a plea for understanding of a political and social climate which allows innocent children to become killers. More than that, it is an attempt to move readers to action, essentially asking them to find ways to end the abhorrent tragedies occurring not just on the African continent, but all over the world.

Character List

Ishmael Beah

The narrator and author of the book. When Beah is a teenager, he spends a year wandering Sierra Leone on the run from the civil war that claims his family. His childhood ended, Beah resorts to survivalist tactics to stay alive; he steals when he needs to, roams in packs of boys his own age who have been orphaned, and he spends long stretches of time alone in the forest. At 13, he is forced to become a soldier for the government's army and is ordered to kill rebels - many of whom are boys his own age. Beah witnesses and perpetrates numerous atrocities before he is rescued and rehabilitated by UNICEF. He speaks at several international conferences on children and war, including one at the United Nations. He currently lives in New York.

Junior

Ishmael Beah's elder brother. Junior is protective of Beah, as he has been for all of the younger boy's life. It is to Junior that Beah looks for reassurance during their trials. Beah is separated from Junior during a rebel attack on Kamator and never sees his older brother again.

Musa

Musa is a Mende boy who was in Mattru Jong when the rebels attacked. Musa and his father were separated from his mother during the attack. Musa's father ordered him to stay where he was until he could return with his wife; as soon as Musa's father returned to the village, the attack grew in intensity and Musa was forced to run. He is among the six boys Beah finds in the forest after his month of isolation. Musa is the storyteller of the group.

Alhaji

Alhaji is a Temne boy who was at the river fetching water when the rebels attacked his village. He returned home to find his family, but all he was able to find was an empty house. Alhaji is among the six boys Beah encounters after his month of isolation in the forest. He remains a close friend of Beah's even as they are rescued together by UNICEF.

Kanei

Kanei is a Mende boy who escaped the rebels' attack on his village with his parents, but lost his two sisters and three brothers in the chaos. He and his parents escape in a boat, but the boat capsized when rebels threw the passengers into panic by shooting at them. Kanei swam to the other side of the river and witnessed many people drowning in the river whiel the rebels laughed at their suffering. He follows the other survivors in the hope of locating his parents, whom others tell him have passed through the area. Kanei is among the six boys Beah encounters after his month of isolation in the forest.

Jumah

Jumah is a Mende boy whose house was destroyed by an RPG during the RUF attack on his village. He runs toward teh wharf to find his parents, but cannot locate them. Along with Moriba, Jumah flees into the forest to find their hiding families, but cannot discover their whereabouts. Jumah is among the six boys Beah encounters after his month of isolation in the forest.

Moriba

Moriba is a Mende boy whose house was destroyed by an RPG during the RUF attack on his village. He runs toward teh wharf to find his parents, but cannot locate them. Along with Jumah, Moriba flees into the forest to find their hiding families, but cannot discover their whereabouts. Moriba is among the six boys Beah encounters after his month of isolation in the forest.

Saidu

Saidu is a Temne boy whose family was unable to leave the village during the rebel attack. He and his family hide under their beds during the night of the attack. The next morning, rebels broke into the house and rape his three sisters. Because he is in the attic retreiving rice for his family at the time, Saidu is safe but is forced to hear the sounds of their suffering as the rebels assault them. The rebels then forced Saidu's parents to pack up and carry their belongings for the rebels depart, taking the sisters with them. Saidu is among the six boys whom Beah encounters following his month of isolation in the forest.

Later, Saidu "faints" when three white-clothed figures--whom the boys believe to be ghosts--pass them in the forest one night. Saidu is catatonic for a long time, but recovers. Unfortunately, he once again slips into this coma when the boys find a welcoming village. That night, Saidu dies.

Lieutenant Jabati

Jabati is Ishmael Beah's commanding officer during his service in the Sierra Leone military. Jabati is known for reading and quoting Shakespeare, particularly *Julius Caesar*; he is also known as an orater who would lecture and exhort his troops for hours in preparation for future combat. Jabati has a flair for the dramatic, once displaying the bodies of a man and his son to the villagers as a deterrent to their fleeing into the forest wehre the rebels are hidden.

Beah comes to trust Jabati as he does no other adult, primarily due to his position of authority and the necessity of such trust to survival. Jabati seemingly betrays Beah by selecting hiim to be among the children taken by UNICEF to be fofered a second chance at normal lives.

Corporal Gadafi

Gadafi is the officer in charge of training the boy soldiers under Lieutenant Jabati. He is tough on the boys, but seems motivated to harshness by a desire to see them survive the armed conflict. He does not hesitate to push the boys beyond their sense of humanity, particularly in the instance where he holds a competition to see which boy can kill a prisoner by cutting his throat the most effectively and quickly.

Uncle Tommy

A relative of Beah's father, Tommy is mentioned almost in passing by Beah when the UNICEF worker Leslie tells him he will be placed in a foster home. Tommy is located and immediately comes to begin developing a relationship with Beah. Although Beah is skeptical of any possible connection at first, Tommy's patience and good humor win Beah over to accepting him as his benefactor.

Uncle Tommy and his wife have no children of their own, but have adopted several children from family members unable to care for their own. Beah is the next to last child taken in (Beah's childhood friend Mohamed is the last) by the family. Uncle Tommy provides a safe environment for Beah to recoup from his trauma; this safety is shattered with a resurgence of violence in Freetown and the eventual death by disease of Uncle Tommy.

Esther

Esther is the nurse at the UNICEF compound where Beah convalesces following his escape from the life as a child soldier. She attempts to win Beah's trust by patiently showing an interest in him without pushing him. She even uses reverse psychology by challenging Beah to win her trust before she will talk with him at length. She learns of Beah's interests through the school questionnaires and uses this knowledge to break down Beah's emotional barriers. She considers Beah a brother and consoles him in his most dismal emotional troubles.

Laura Simms

Laura Simms is a facilitator for the United Nations First Children's Parliament; her workshop is intended to help the children learn more effective ways of communicating their harrowing experiences to their audience. Beah connects with her immediately because she is a storyteller and he comes from a culture strong in storytelling roots. Laura eventually adopts Beah as her son when he escapes the resurgence of violence in Sierra Leone.

Gibrilla

Gibrilla is one of the boys who accompanies Beah and Junior after they are forced to leave Mattru Jong.

Talloi

Talloi is with Junior and Beah when they initially go to Mattru Jong to practice with their dance group. After the rebel attacks, Talloi is among the group of six boys that travel together until the siege of Kamator.

Kaloko

Kaloko travels among the group of six boys from Mattru Jong through Kamator.

Khalilou

Beah, Junior, Talloi, Kaloko, and Gibrilla stay with Khalilou's family in Mattru Jong after the attack on their village. Khalilou's family leaves them to watch the house when the rebels are rumored to have targeted Mattru Jong. These six boys stay together until Kamator is raided.

Mohamed

Beah's best friend before the war. He is unable to travel with the his friends to Mattru Jong for the dance group practice, so he is present when the rebels attack Mogbwemo. Amazingly, Beah is reunited with Mohamed years later at the UNICEF rehabilitation camp.

Father

Before the war, Beah has a complicated relationship with his father. He is a carefree man, invested in the futures of his sons. However, a relationship with a new woman has soured the relationship with his Ishmael and Junior. Still, Beah has fond memories of his father that he comfort him during his ordeal. He is presumed dead.

Mother

Beah's mother loves her sons despite the divorce that has torn their family apart. Beah recalls visits with his mother and brother Ibrahim, trips to the market, and her teaching him how to cook during his ordeal. She is presumed dead.

Mamie Kpana

Ishmael's grandmother. Mamie Kpana is a calm presence in Beah's pre-war life.

Ibrahim

Beah's younger brother. He lives with their mother following their parents' divorce. Ibrahim attends school unlike his brothers, as his mother is solely devoted to his upbringing. After the attack on Mogbwemo, Beah never sees Ibrahim again.

Sheku

Sheku is a tent-mate of Beah's at the army-occupied village. They become soldiers together.

Josiah

Josiah is a tent-mate of Beah's when he becomes a soldier. Josiah dies of a broken back during one of their first raids.

Gasemu

Gasemu recognizes Beah from Mattru Jong. When they arrive to the outskirts of the village where it is rumored his parents have taken refuge in, Gasemu greets the boys. Instead of letting Beah run on to the village, he makes them help him carry bananas. While they are walking on to the village, rebels attack and all are killed. Beah blames Gasemu for keeping him from his family, though he comes to realize that it is not his fault and he is alive, once again, because of a twist of fate.

Mr. Kamara

The head of Benin Home who encourages Beah to speak publicly about his experiences.

Leslie

A kind worker at Benin Home.

Aunt Sallay

Uncle Tommy's wife. She treats Beah like her own son.

Allie

Uncle Tommy's son. Beah and Allie share a room after Beah leaves Benin Home. Allie takes Beah to a dance and gives him city clothes as a way to introduce him to his new, post-war life.

Dr. Tamba

The sponsor from Sierra Leone who accompanies Beah and Bah to New York City.

Bah

A Sierra Leonean boy who travels with Beah to represent their country at the UN.

Major Themes

Survival

From the moment he fled the violence at Mattru Jong, the focus of Beah's life became surviving day to day. He learns quickly that in order to survive, he must suppress his true emotions. After the RUF attacks Mattru Jong, Beah lets go of his prior attachments to family and friends, joining up with boys who, like him, are on the run. Even though he welcomes the company, he remains emotionally distant from his newfound friends. When they die or become separated from one another, Beah does not have time to mourn. His goal is to live through one more day, and he can't afford to stop and think about the atrocities around him.

For months, Beah stays alive by overcoming hunger, violence and isolation. When Beah becomes a soldier, he is trained to tap into his rage in order to kill rebels. The officers manipulate the boys into thinking they are exacting revenge on the people who killed their families. Beah acknowledges it is unlikely that he and his fellow soldiers confront those actually responsible for their families' deaths, but the temptation to believe is strong. They accept this as reality - fueled by drugs and violent films - and operate on the assumption that they kill or be killed.

When Beah arrives at Benin Home, he finds it hard to access his true feelings about the loss and the violence he has experienced. After years of subverting his emotions, he is unable or unwilling to speak about what happened because Beah long gave up hope for a real life. Only through therapy is he able to trust others begin to tell his story. Cutting off his emotions kept him alive, but examining those feelings after the war gave him a new life.

Memory

Beah weaves memories of his life before the war into his recounting of months on the run from the RUF. In distressing times, Beah calls up happier moments in order to get through another day. Memories of his family - especially those of times before his parents divorced - allow him to keep a glimmer of hope alive in the darkness. His memories of his grandfather help in a more direct way; Beah uses legends and advice from his childhood while alone in the forest. Memory is an aid. When he becomes a soldier, however, Beah no longer indulges in memories of his childhood. After he kills his first man, the memories become a burden as he believes his life will never be the same. When he is rescued by UNICEF, he still resists remembering his family because he is afraid he will have to first reexamine his war years in order to access memories from before. But, Beah uses flashbacks later in the book as he allows his memories to return while he is in rehabilitation. For Beah, memory is the key to survival at the start of the war, then blotted out as a coping mechanism when he is forced to do inhuman things, and a signifier of healing later on.

Loss of Innocence

Obviously, since Beah became a child soldier, his tale would incorporate the resulting loss of innocence. The violence and terror is rendered through the eyes of a child and Beah writes plainly and without judgment about his experiences. Though the attacks on his village and subsequent villages he seeks haven in sever Beah from normal childhood activities, he at first maintains his innocence. He holds onto childhood memories and is able to fleetingly rekindle his sense of wonder; for example, he and his companions rejoice when they first see the ocean.

Although the violent pursuit of rebels across Sierra Leone traumatized Beah, it is not until he is turned into a killer that he truly loses his innocence. To emphasize this change narratively, Beah stops utilizing flashbacks to his childhood in the memoir after he is indoctrinated into the army, citing his inability to remember anything good. Beah details the manipulative tactics used by the commanding officers to create killers, which have the cumulative effect of eradicating childlike emotions or actions. Beah's experiences in the war strip him of his humanity but the relief efforts help restore the dreams he had forsaken when he was 12.

Nature

Even amid the horrors of civil war, Beah can see a grander perspective when confronted by natural beauty. Beah strives to be like the moon, he is adept at living off of the forest when he is stranded, and he rejoices when he sees the ocean for the first time. In nature, Beah retains his innocence. In his memoir, nature also echoes or foreshadows coming evil. Left alone in Mattru Jong after most of the villagers fled to the forest, Beah notes that the moon does not appear in the sky that night and that the air felt "stiff, as if nature itself was afraid of what was happening." (p. 22) When Beah is traveling with Kanei, Musa, Alhaji, Saidu, Jumah and Moriba, a crow falls out of the sky and the boys, desperately hungry, eat it despite their ominous feelings. The next day, Saidu falls ill and dies shortly thereafter.

For Beah, there's a deeper spirit to nature, one that resists the manmade atrocity. As a soldier, when it rains, he notes that the forest is washed clean, "as if the soil had refused to absorb anymore blood for that day." (p. 150) When his rehabilitation starts to take hold, Beah considers the moon for the first time since the war. For the past several years leading up to this moment, Beah has been divorced from the redemptive power of nature. He has been trained to fight, to kill, and to survive. Now, having broken through his own barriers against trusting nurse Esther and the UNICEF worker Leslie, Beah recovers his sense of family history. He invokes the memory of his grandmother and her lesson about man's communion with the natural world. For the first time since he was inducted into the army, Beah remembers this connection and seeks to make himself whole again.

Life and Hope

Hope comes in the starkest terms for Beah during his ordeal. When on the run from the RUF, Beah is able to comfort himself with memories of his earlier life. His father's saying, "If you are alive, there is hope for a better day and something good to happen. If there is nothing good left in the destiny of a person, he or she will die" is enough to push him towards another day. (p. 54) Being alive one more day is proof that all is not yet lost.

When he is a soldier, however, Beah forfeits a connection to his life. Hope dims in the haze of drugs and violence. Beah gives up any dream of a future beyond simply surviving. However, his father's adage rings true once rehabilitation begins. After speaking at the UN, Beah's hope is rekindled. He meets many children like him and sees that his experiences can have an impact on the world. For once, he realizes that someone will care if he lives or dies. Far away from the civil war, Beah's life has meaning again. In New York, also meets storyteller Laura Simms who offers him a lifeline out of Sierra Leone - which he eventually takes.

The Damages of War

Beah's memoir sheds light on the multifaceted damage done by civil war and terrorism. The anguish of losing his family and friends is compounded by the uncertainty each day brings. Although they attempt to find a safe haven from the war, the boys know from bitter experience that no such place seems to exist in Sierra Leone. Each new village brings either hopelessness - in the form of desolation and isolation - or hostility on the part of the frightened inhabitants. Beah feels that there is no place for him to call "home" any longer, and fears that such a place may never exist in his future. Whatever dreams or goals he had set no longer seem possible.

As a soldier, the fear subsides and he is forced to tap into rage and vengeance in order to survive. The constant violent acts Beah is subjected, as well as the drugs he becomes addicted to, tamp down his fear - but also his humanity. The war also breaks down civilization. Beah notes that before the war, kids his age would never raise their voice against adults. But the rebels and soldiers respect no one. Because of this, when Beah travels in packs of other lost boys, they are assumed to be devils. The civil war leads to chaos and mistrust on both personal and community levels.

Family

Beah loses his mother, father, brothers and grandparents in the war. Family is the most important thing for Beah, and he struggles to keep his family alive any way he can. At first, he is stranded along with his brother Junior in Mattru Jong. Their bond deepens despite the tragedy that has befallen them. Ishmael and Junior try to protect each other as best they can, as they had when they were "misfits" at school. However, when they become separated, Beah is unable to mourn for him as he must focus on staying alive.

Each pack of boys Beah ends up with during his travels becomes an ad hoc family; family becomes situational rather than genetic. But each boy realizes that something irreplaceable has been lost. When Saidu dies, Kanei must represent his family at the funeral. The villager who accompanies them say that they will always know where their friend is buried and can return; but each boy knows they will never return. Later, Beah's squad becomes his family. Even at Benin Home, the ex-RUF boys clash with the rescued army boys. Likely orphaned, each boy desperately clings to one another. Family is something to fight for.

At Benin Home, Esther offers to be Beah's sister but he can only grant her familial status on a temporary basis. He has been jaded by war, but he still seeks connection. Beah eventually finds a home with Uncle Tommy - who, like Beah during the war, takes care of children other than his own despite not being blood - but he is wary of opening up about his wartime experiences. Beah does not want to alienate his cousins. Beah has learned that family is precious but can be fleeting.

The memories and stories of Beah's childhood are interspersed throughout the memoir, typically at times when Beah is most afraid. Within the story, they are a comfort to child Beah, but they also serve a greater, narrative purpose. With Esther, Beah bemoans the fact that as sole survivor, no one else will be able to tell stories of his childhood. His memoir is a way to keep his family alive in some way.

Glossary of Terms

AK-47

a selective-fire, gas-operated 7.62×39mm assault rifle, first developed in the Soviet Union by Mikhail Kalashnikov; its relative cheapness and the ease of replacing parts made it a common weapon in various third-world conflicts such as the Sierra Leone civil war

brown brown

cocaine mixed with gunpowder; a common drug used by the soldiers in the military as a cheap high both during and between combat encounters

calabash

a fruit which can either be harvested while young and used as a vegetable, or harvested mature, dried, and used as a bottle.

carseloi

Mende for "spider," a name Ishmael Beah's grandmother gives him due to his tricky nature.

cassava

also called yuca or manioc, cassava is a woody shrub of the Euphorbiaceae family native to South America; it is a staple of many diets for its ability to thrive in tropical climates and its starchy content.

crapes

African word for sneakers

cutlass

A short sword with a slightly curved blade

G3

a 7.62mm battle rifle developed in the 1950s by the German armament manufacturer Heckler & Koch GmbH (H&K) in collaboration with the Spanish state-owned design and development agency CETME; the G3 is one of the main weapons used by both the RUF and the Sierra Leone military during their civil war

gari

grated dried fruit made from cassava

hammock

a hanging length of netting or fabric, attached to two supports, used as a bed or seat

imam

the prayer leader of a mosque

kola nut

the nut of the kola tree, a genus of trees native to the tropical rainforests of Africa

Krio

the de facto national language spoken throughout the West African nation of Sierra Leone

lappei

a large cotton cloth worn by many African women around their waists.

leweh

rice paste, a mixture used both in secular dining and religiously-themed cermonies

lorry

British word for truck; used in Sierra Leone due to the British influence on the English dialect spoken there.

Mende

a major language of Sierra Leone, with some speakers in neighboring Liberia. It is spoken both by the Mende people and by other ethnic groups

migraine

severe headache often accompanied by nausea, vomiting, and visual impairment

palampo

African word for "single," as in unmarried. Beah's mother teaches him to cook so that he can eat during his single (palampo) life, but immediately becomes sober and asks him to marry so that she may have grandchildren.

repatriated

restored to one's country of birth or original citizenship

RPG

Rocket-Propelled Grenade. A hand-held weapon capable of delivering a grenade great distances and to devastating effect. The rebels in Sierra Leone use RPGs often to terrorize villages, as they are effective both against people, property, and vehicles.

RUF

The Revolutionary United Front, the name the rebels have given their movement. The initials "RUF" are carved into select captives by the rebels in order to recruit them to their cause; victims of this mutilation cannot escape rebel detection if they flee, and are often seen as rebel sympathizers by the citizens and government forces.

skepticism

attitude of doubt or suspicion

sleepers

African term for flip-flops.

soukous

a dance music genre that originated in the two neighbouring countries of Belgian Congo and French Congo during the 1930s and early 1940s, and which has gained popularity throughout Africa

sura

Any of the 114 chapters or sections of the Koran

tarp

short for tarpaulin, a heavy fabric used as a covering for shelters and tents

thatch

noun--plant material such as palm fronds used as roofing material;

verb--to use plant material to cover and insulate a roof

verandah

a roofed opened gallery or porch

wahlee

a place outside villages where people processed coffee or other crops

Short Summary

A Long Way Gone begins in Ishmael Beah's early youth in 1993. A twist of fate leads Beah (along with his older brother and two friends) to leave their home village to practice for a talent competition in a nearby town on the eve of an attack by the Revolutionary United Front (RUF) on his home village of Mogbwemo. From that moment, chaos envelops Beah's life as he seeks news of his family and survival for himself and his companions.

Early in the RUF assaults, Beah learns of the rebels' horrific actions mostly through hearsay and rumor. He spends the first few chapters of the book attempting to find his way home but when he learns "home" has been wiped out, he seeks information about his family's well-being. Beah, his brother Junior, and his friends form a small party of survivors seeking to return to the peace they had once known. Even at this point, the RUF attacks have turned Beah from child to young adult whose priorities have shifted from a love of rap music to a need to survive through each day's difficulties.

Beah and his companions run into the rebels and are separated from one another. Alone, Beah comes to grips with dangers both physical (snakes, wild boars, food supply) and psychological (isolation and fear). He reunites with his previous companions only to discover that the village he believed the rest of his family to have taken refuge in has already been hit by the RUF and utterly destroyed.

Now deprived of hope that his family will ever be whole again, Beah is ripe for indoctrination into the government military structure. He is taken to a government camp and treated well at first; however, it becomes clear that the government is facing too strong an opposition in the RUF and must now recruit boys into its army. As part of their conditioning, the boys are given drugs (cocaine and marijuana), fed a steady diet of American action films (such as *Rambo: First Blood*), and rewarded for finding the most efficient way to kill an enemy.

For nearly three years, Beah becomes the very thing that appalled him before: a bloodthirsty, heartless killer. He and his unit commit the same atrocities that the RUF had perpetrated upon Beah's own village and neighboring towns. Beah becomes desensitized to his situation, living each day in a haze of drug-induced apathy and regimented bloodlust.

UNICEF intervenes, taking some of the more "promising" boys away from their life of military violence. At first, Beah cannot reconcile himself to the seemingly weak ways of the foreign UNICEF workers and the locals who interact with him at the UNICEF camp. Only through the constant efforts of Esther, a UNICEF nurse, to treat him as a human being, not a monster, is Beah able to reconnect with his emotional self and grieve the terrors he has both undergone and committed.

Beah is sent to live with his Uncle Tommy and his family in Freetown - then unaffected by the war. He struggles to assimilate among people who are happy all the time. He is unable to speak about his experiences out of fear of alienating his new-found connections.

Beah learns of an opportunity to speak to the United Nations and strives to obtain one of two spots on the delegation to be sent from Sierra Leone to New York City. Through perseverence, Beah obtains the position and is flown to the United States to address the UN in person. He marvels at New York City by night and is trained to better tell his story by day. Eventually, he speaks before the General Assembly, moving the UN delegates to take action condemning the RUF and seeking to aid the people of Sierra Leone. His speaking instructor Laura Simms gives him her contact information in case he ever needs more help.

When he returns to Freetown, the city is invaded by a combination of the army and the RUF. Many people die, including Beah's Uncle, and Beah himself does not think he is able of surviving another experience of war. Beah leaves his family again and becomes a refugee. He escapes to neighboring Guinea and contacts Laura Simms. Eventually, she adopts him and he relocates to the United States, where he completes his secondary education and eventually attends college.

Quotes and Analysis

These days I live in three worlds: my dreams, and the experiences of my new life, which trigger memories from the past.

Ishmael Beah, p. 20

After a month of living in the relative safety of New York City, Ishmael Beah is still haunted by nightmares of his time fighting the war in Sierra Leone. His new life is unfamiliar to him and cannot protect him from returning to the past terrors of his young life. Worse still, his vivid dreams constantly draw him back to the terror of his life in Sierra Leone as a victim of the RUF violence. He is a young man divided against himself, as his country had been divided against itself - in both cases, due to the rebels' violent actions.

Things changed rapidly in a matter of seconds and no one had any control over anything. We had yet to learn these things and implement survival tactics, which was what it came down to.

Ishmael Beah, p. 29

Beah acknowledges that the rebels' violence has force himself and others like him to resort to "survival tactics." His world has been turned upside-down, and in the shock of his first few months' experience with the civil war, he is not yet ready to change with the mercurial situations he finds himself in. When civilization breaks down, the world is thrown into chaos and former priorities are set aside in favor of mere survival. Beah here foreshadows that he will eventually learn that life-saving lesson, but hints that it is a deplorable situation for a young man be forced to turn all his thought to survival from day to day.

When I was very little, my father used to say, "If you are alive, there is hope for a better day and something good to happen. If there is nothing good left in the destiny of a person, he or she will die."

Ishmael Beah, pg. 54

Beah's recollection of his father's words helps him to keep pushing forward, even though he is lost in the forest without a purpose in life. He is able to hold onto this precept even as he battles depression brought on by his isolation from other human beings. It is this lesson that keeps Beah moving onward even when horrible things happen to him and those around him; he believes that his destiny will still have some good in it so long as he is alive. Conversely, he knows that his life will end when he has run out of good fortune, so he has no fear of pushing forward toward whatever life has in store for him.

My eyes widened, a smile forming on my face. Even in the middle of the madness there remained that true and natural beauty, and it took my mind away from my current situation as I marveled at this sight.

Ishmael Beah, p. 59

Even amid the horrors of civil war, Beah can see a grander perspective when confronted by natural beauty. He and his companions had never seen the ocean, so the sight, sound, and smell of it overwhelms them with joy. For the first time since any of them fled the rebels, they joke with one another, wrestle in fun, and play soccer on the beach. The boys have a moment of respite from their terrifying ordeal, and in that moment remind the reader (and each other) that they are still children at heart, forced to grow up too quickly because of circumstances beyond their control.

One of the unsettling things about my journey, mentally, physically, and emotionally, was that I wasn't sure when or where it was going to end. I didn't know what I was going to do with my life. I felt that I was starting over and over again.

Ishmael Beah, p. 69

Beah's memoir sheds light on the multifaceted damage done by civil war and terrorism. As a victim of the violence, a young man who has lost his family and way of life and is in turn considered dangerous by most of the civilians he encounters, Beah suffers more than simiple physical pain. The anguish of losing his family and friends is compounded by the uncertainty each day brings. Although they attempt to find a safe haven, the boys know from bitter experience that no such place seems to exist in Sierra Leone. Each new village brings either hopelessness - in the form of desolation and isolation - or hostility on the part of the frightened inhabitants. Beah feels that there is no place for him to call "home" any longer, and fears that such a place may never exist in his future. He must start "over and over again" with each new day, keep moving so as to avoid both the rebels and their terrified victims. For Beah, as for any other refugee from warfare, there can be no rest. Whatever dreams he had in childhood of his adult life have not only been put on hold, they have been obliterated. His only goal now is to live through each day.

That morning we thanked the men who had helped bury Saidu. "You will always know where he is laid," one of the men said. I nodded in agreement, but I know that the chances of coming back to the village were slim, as we had no control over our future. We know only how to survive.

Ishmael Beah, p. 87

Despite their acceptance by villagers and refugees, Beah and his companions suffer the loss of one of their own - the coma-stricken Saidu. Their place in the village is confirmed by the sorrowful ceremony of Saidu's funeral, a rite of passage heralding both belonging and loss. Despite their kindness in the wake of tragedy, Beah knows that he and his friends cannot find peace among the villagers. They have changed too drastically on the inside; they have grown up too quickly into men who recognize that survival is more important than familial connections. Unfortunately for the boys, their losses to date have hardened them into people who exist only to keep existing, with no higher purpose in mind.

Whenever I looked at rebels during raids, I got angrier, because they looked like the rebels who played cards in the ruins of the village where I had lost my family. So when the lieutenant gave orders, I shot as many as I could, but I didn't feel any better.

Ishmael Beah, p. 122

Beah sums up his coping mechanism and motivation for becoming an effective killer in the Sierra Leone civil war. He channels his pain at the loss of his family into a raging hatred of the rebels who killed his loved ones, and lets the fire of this anger burn through his gunfire. Even as he uses this method to dehumanize his enemies, he realizes that killing an infinite number of rebels will not restore his soul to peace, nor will it reclaim his lost childhood. He follows orders, and follows them effectively, but his humanity is the price he must pay for being a good soldier.

I had my gun now, and as the corporal always said, "This gun is your source of power in these times. It will protect you and provide you all you need, if you know how to use it well."

Ishmael Beah, p. 124

Corporal Gadafi's mentality is demonstrated by this statement, which the corporal transmits to the soldiers under his command. In the violent times of the Sierra Leone civil war, weapons are power; Beah learns to focus his sense of security and strength in his G3 rifle for most of his military career. Later in the memoir, when his weapon is taken from him, he panics and feels at a loss without the tool of violence which has come to define him.

This emphasis on the power of the object is central to the soldiers' ability to cope with the chaos of the civil war. In a world where lives may be lost seemingly at random, and death may come from almost any direction, the only power any soldier has to control the world around him resides in his gun. Like so many other soldiers, Beah must accept this reality in order to survive and remain relatively sane in the violent nightmare landscape of constant ambushes, raids, and sudden deaths.

Sometimes we were asked to leave for war in the middle of a movie. We would come back hours later after killing many people and continue the movie as if we had just returned from intermission. we were always either at the front lines, watching a war movie, or doing drugs. There was no time to be alone or to think.

Ishmael Beah, p. 124

Another coping mechanism used by the soldiers was desensitization. By believing that armed conflict was as much a part of daily life as mealtime or movies, the men are able to shut off their feelings about the death and suffering they see (and create). The movies serve to desensitize them further; they watch violent films such as *Rambo* and *Commando* which glorify and stylize violence to the point that the viewers can create a disconnect between their actions and the real world.

Beah's comment that "There was no time to be alone or think" hints at what he later terms "brainwashing" on the part of the military structure. The soldiers are given no chance to reflect on their actions, lest they begin to comprehend the full scope of their deeds and their surroundings. By keeping the men busy, entertained, or drugged, the officers are able to keep their men steady for the job they must do: kill rebels. The cost is the soldiers' humanity.

When I was a child, my grandmother told me that the sky speaks to those who look and listen to it. She said, "In the sky there are always answers and explanations for everything: every pain, every suffering, joy, and confusion." That night I wanted the sky to talk to me.

Ishmael Beah, p. 166

Beah makes this statement in Chapter 17, immediately after repeating his fascination with the appearance of the moon in Chapter 1. The sky again represents the natural world - the world greater than that of civil strife and human violence. For the past several years leading up to this moment, Beah has been divorced from the redemptive power of nature. He has been trained to fight, to kill, and to survive. Now, having broken through his own barriers against trusting nurse Esther and the UNICEF worker Leslie, Beah recovers his sense of family history. He invokes the memory of his grandmother and her lesson about man's communion with the natural world. For the first time since he was inducted into the army, Beah remembers this connection and seeks to make himself whole again.

Summary and Analysis of Prologue: New York City, 1998

Summary

Beah, here 18, introduces his memoir with a brief exchange of dialogue with his high school friends, who don't fully grasp the weight of his experiences in Sierra Leone. His friends respond "cool" when he confirms that he had witnessed combat. Beah smiles a little but won't tell them anything more about his childhood.

Analysis

This quick exchange sets the tone of Beah's memoir. As a teenager in New York City, Beah is gained a few years' distance from his traumatic experiences in Sierra Leone, yet he is still unable or unwilling to to into detail with his friends. This is a constant struggle for Beah; though he later speaks at the UN about the atrocities he witnessed, he is reluctant to share memories of his own violent deeds - to spare himself both pain and alienation.

Beah wrote his memoir when he was 27. As an adult, he is finally able to reconcile his actions and share his story. Instead of clamming up when faced with questions from people who couldn't possibly understand what he went through, Beah decides to try to make them understand through his own words. In the Prologue, he adopts a style that mimics his 18-year-old thoughts. The rest of the Chapters are written in a similar, age-appropriate tone.

Summary and Analysis of Chapter 1

Summary

Beah begins the memoir by describing how unreal rumors of the war seem to his ten-year-old world. His view of war, he states, had been colored by "those that I had read about in books or seen in movies such as Rambo: First Blood" (p. 5). Two years later, in January of 1993, the war hits home for him when Ishmael, his friend Talloi and brother Junior visit the village of Mattru Jong to see some old friends and practice their rap group performance for an upcoming talent show. The local friends arrive home early with the news that school has been cancelled since Mogbwemo, Beah's home sixteen miles away, has been attacked by rebels. One Mattru Jong friend, Gibrilla, states that the teachers believe Mattru Jong itself will be the rebels' next target. Despite this possibility, many refugees from Mobwembo flee to Mattru Jong; therefore, Beah and his friends go to the nearby wharf to await the incoming people and look for their families among the refugees. When no one they know arrives after several hours, the boys decide to head back to Mogbwemo to find their families. Ishmael is concerned about his Father, Mother and younger brother Ibrahim. (His parents are divorced).

En route to Mogbwemo, the boys stop at Kabati, the village of Beah's grandmother Mamie Kpana, just as they had on their outbound trip. In contrast to the earlier hospitality they had received by Beah's grandmother, the deserted village offers nothing but ominous silence. When evening arrives, so do several people who had evacuated to the nearby mining area. Beah is struck by the sound of crying children looking for their parents and babies wailing for food; he also sees adults bleeding, vomiting and reacting with hysteria to the catastrophe that has befallen them. As the boys debate the wisdom of returning to the site of the rebel attack, they see a mother carrying her dead baby on her back. She stops to take the baby in her arms - bullets are visible in the infant's body - and cradles it, too shocked to shed tears for her dead child. This incident forces the boys to resolve that Mogbwemo is no longer livable and so they decide to return to Mattru Jong.

In Mattru Jong, Beah is reunited with his grandmother. The boys all take up residence there and spend every morning at the wharf seeking news about their missing families and the war. The boys distract themselves by memorizing American rap lyrics from Ishmael's cassettes. An old man encourages Beah that they should "be like the moon". When Ishmael asks his grandmother what this means, she explains that even though people complain when the sun shines too brightly, no one is annoyed by the brightness of the moon. Good things happen when the moon is full and its light is at its greatest. Beah remembers his own experiences as a six-year-old boy, lying on the ground at night looking up at the moon. He remembers the various images he saw in the moon, and in recalling this pleasant memory from his childhood, he is encouraged.

Analysis

Ishmael Beah takes a matter-of-fact tone in his memoir. Although he is recounting great horrors experienced by his twelve-year-old self, he does not dwell on lurid details or seem to exaggerate for dramatic effect. He states plainly what he sees and what he thinks, allowing the reader to reach his or her own conclusions regarding the rebel attack on his home village of Mogbwemo.

While taking an objective stance, Beah nonetheless makes use of narrative techniques in his writing. Foremost among them is his use of flashbacks to give necessary background to an impending scene (and also to heighten tension). In the section he begins with "The first time that I was touched by war I was twelve" (p. 6), he immediately launches into a flashback detailing the origin of his rap group conceived by himself and his friends Talloi and Mohamed and his older brother Junior. This gives the reader important information regarding Beah's motive for walking to neighboring Mattru Jong on the day his own village is attacked by rebels. The boys are immersed in the western culture of rap music and oblivious to the dangers of violence posed by the rebel factions in Sierra Leone. In this way, Beah is able to connect his experience more universally to others whose childhood experiences consist of acts of leisure, such as learning the lyrics to pop music and imitating their favorite entertainers.

This flashback, as well as later ones involving a visit to his mother and the last time he saw his father, heighten the poignancy and confusion birthed by the rebel attack on Mogbwemo. Beah was not ready for such a drastic change in his world, so he and his friends find themselves in shock for several days following the news of his village's destruction. The loss of his family numbs him as he attempts to assimilate how tragically and catastrophically his world has changed. By the end of the chapter, he is still hopeful that something good will happen, and that the violence will end soon.

Summary and Analysis of Chapter 2

Summary

Chapter 2 opens with Beah pushing a wheelbarrow toward a cemetery. The wheelbarrow holds a dead body, wrapped in white. Beah is now an experienced soldier, carrying his AK-47 on his back as he pushes his blood-stained cargo toward its destination. He wonders why this body is going to the cemetery when so many others have been left to die where they fell or be buried elsewhere. Once he stops, he unwraps the body feet first, uncovering myriad bullet wounds all over the corpse. When he reaches the face, he discovers that it is his own.

He awakens to his new life in New York City. He has only been here a month, so his surroundings upon awakening are still unfamiliar to him. He cannot shake the dream-memory of his time in Sierra Leone. He reflects that he now lives in three worlds: the present, his dreams, and the past.

Analysis

Beah opens this chapter by jumping in time past his experiences in the civil war. In his dream, he is a hardened soldier, inured to death. The change in Beah is jarring compared to the optimistic boy of Chapter 1, who recalled childhood images of the moon that made him happy. When he reaches the point of discovering the corpse is his own, the reader understands that this is a dream - but it is a dream informed by horrid memory. The reader is then told that Beah lives in New York City, in his "new life". This sets the stage for hope: we know that whatever Beah experiences throughout the violence of Sierra Leone, he will arrive safely in New York City. However, that safety is only physical; he is still haunted by memories and nightmare scenes of the violence he saw while still so young.

The dream image of Beah pushing his own corpse in the wheelbarrow foreshadows the death of his youthful innocence when he acts in accordance with his commanding officer's order to kill a prisoner. He finds himself the agent of his own symbolic death and with that knowledge must deal with the attenuating grief.

Beah's trifold world - past, present, and dreams - will continue to overlap throughout the book, with the primary emphasis placed upon the past (which really forms the narrative's "present" throughout). Memories, usually in the form of dreams, will mitigate the horrors Beah encounters throughout his youth during the Sierra Leone civil war. In the current chapter, however, the reader is simply introduced to the horrors of Beah's life as a boy soldier through the metaphorical language of dreams and as a past belonging to a different place and time, and thus physically separate from the Beah of the present. This serves to distance both Beah and the reader from the horrors which are about to be recounted, ironically making the full scope of the atrocities more comprehensible.

Summary and Analysis of Chapter 3

Summary

Chapter 3 returns to the primary narrative thread established in Chapter 1. Beah and his brother and friends remain in Mattru Jong longer than anticipated due to the lack of news of their families and the continued violence. Rumors abound that the rebels are planning to attack Mattru Jong; these rumors are heightened by letters from nearby Sumbuya, a town whose inhabitants were largely massacred by the rebels, indicating that the rebels would be coming to Mattru Jong and expected to be welcomed by the people they were supposedly fighting for. One messenger arrives with all of his fingers except for his thumbs cut off - a mutilation called "one love" by the rebels in mockery of the Sierra Leonean custom of raising a thumb and saying "one love" in imitation of reggae music culture. This same messenger has the initials RUF carved into his body to mark him as belonging to the rebels (the "Revolutionary United Front").

The arrival of this messenger leads the people of Mattru Jong to go into hiding in the forest; Khalilou's family, with whom Beah and his companions are staying, ask the young men to follow them with the family possessions if the situation did not improve soon. The largely deserted town becomes a frightening environment to Beah, who discovers that it is the people who give life to a town.

Most of the inhabitants of Mattru Jong remained in hiding for a week. More messengers arrive, indicating the approach of the rebels, which leads even more of the people to seek shelter outside the town. Again, Beah and his companions are left behind to tend Khalilou's family's home.

Beah is again surprised by violence as the rebels arrive while he is cooking. He and his young friends hear gunshots, and the attack ensues. Chaos takes over as the rebels fire their rifles into the sky, frightening the people into fleeing. Beah heads to the Mattru Jong soldiers' encampment which he assumes will be the safest place to hide, only to discover that the soldiers foresaw the attack and have already deserted the town. The rebels push the people of Mattru Jong toward the river, leaving only a path through a muddy swamp as an escape route; the people are in such a panic that the wounded and disabled are left to die. At this point the rebels begin shooting into the crowds, as they want the people to remain in the village as hostages and potential recruits. Beah and his friends know that, as young boys, they are at greatest risk for forced recruitment: the rebels have a practice of capturing young boys and carving the initials RUF into their bodies to mark them for future use and to turn civilians and government soldiers against them. Beah, Junior, Talloi, Gibrilla, Kaloko, and Khalilou flee into the forest and escape with their lives.

Analysis

The surprise at the rebels' violence - even after repeated warnings that the rebels were approaching - stands out in Beah's account. He attempts to maintain a regular, everyday pattern of living even as he is maintaining a home for people who have taken shelter in the forest out of fear of the rebels. That Beah and his friends, as both outsiders to Mattru Jong and as young men, are asked to remain behind shows the fear and callousness of the terrified citizens of Mattru Jong.

The rebels' tactics are described in detail, giving the reader a picture of their bloody practices and cruel humor. That they send mutilated messengers demanding that the people remain in the town shows their ability to use psychological tricks to frighten the inhabitants of the town, and suggests a bitter irony as they expect hospitality at the hands of their soon-to-be hostages. Beah notes that the rebels prefer to keep mostly women and children in the villages they attack, in order to delay military action on the part of the government. Though repugnant in their bloodthirstiness, the rebels' plans are nonetheless diabolically effective.

Summary and Analysis of Chapter 4

Summary

Chapter 4 continues the narrative from where Chapter 3 left off. Beah and his companions walk for several days in their efforts to escape the rebels. As hunger begins to afflict them, they search abandoned villages for food, but find little worth eating. Soon they decide that the only way to get food is to return to Mattru Jong for their money so that they can buy some at the first market they find.

The boys make the dangerous visit to Mattru Jong, ever-alert to rebel presence. Once they are all ready to depart, they carefully break into groups to cross the open area along the marsh between the village and the cover of the forest. Beah's group makes it across, then Beah discovers the reason for their caution: a handful of rebels are on watch nearby. Beah's brother Junior is in the next group; they are nearly discovered when someone drops something out of his pocket onto a pot, breaking the silence. Junior and the others pretend to be corpses, and nearby gunfire in the village distracts the rebels so that the boys are able to make it to the forest undetected. Another group includes a boy carrying a large sack of belongings; the sack becomes stuck between some tree roots and he is discovered by the rebels. Despite the urging of the others, the boy remains with the sack in a vain attempt to dislodge it and flee with it; the boy is caught by the rebels and those already across escape into the forest.

The boys are delighted at their second escape from Mattru Jong, this time with money, but face disappointment when they reach a nearby village. Despite the smell of cooking food, there is nothing to eat available for sale as the villagers are saving the food for themselves in case their fortunes take a turn for the worst. That night the boys turn to stealing others' food in order to survive the night.

Analysis

Beah describes the increasing breakdown of civilization throughout the region. The return to Mattru Jong was dangerous and, in the end, futile because the rebels' terrorizing influence has reached beyond their immediate presence to the nearby villages. Civilians everywhere are now so frightened of what may happen to them that they close themselves off to others. Beah himself notes that the desperate circumstances lead him and his companions to resort to stealing food because "[it] was the only way to get through the night" (p. 29). Beah recognizes that this is not a choice he would make under normal conditions, but that his world is changing so rapidly he must adapt as quickly as he can to survive.

Summary and Analysis of Chapter 5

Summary

Beah and his companions experience hunger and thirst the likes of which none of them had encountered before. They scavenge abandoned farms and even stooped to assaulting a little boy who had two boiled ears of corn to himself. The boy's parents, rather than confronting the young men, instead give them each an ear of corn; Beah assumes pity saved them from punishment. Beah feels guilty about their pillage, but accepts that they had no other option.

As they continue on their journey, Beah, his brother Junior, and their friends Gibrilla, Kaloko, Talloi and Khalilou are captured by rebels "none of whom," Beah notes "were older than twenty-one" (p. 31). The six boys are taken to a nearby rebel-occupied village, all the time threatened with being shot by their guard should they step out of line. While being held there, Beah witnesses the rebels' torment of an old man who wanders into the village looking for his family. The rebels knock the old man to the ground and threaten to run a bayonet through his throat while they interrogate him. They accuse the old man of being unsympathetic to their cause, then fire a gun next to his head, convincing the old man (temporarily) that he has been shot. The rebels laugh at the desperate old man's antics, and force the boys to laugh as well, at gunpoint.

Beah, his friends, and some other captured boys are then lined up to be selected for initiation into the RUF. The rebels' first round picks include Khalilou, Beah, and a few others, but some rebels protest that the choosing was done poorly and they start over. This second time Junior is chosen but Beah and his friends are not. Junior and the other chosen boys are then told by the rebels that they will be initiated into the RUF through the trial of killing the boys who were not chosen. Junior nearly bursts into tears at the thought of killing the boys, but nearby gunshots disrupt the proceedings and the boys manage to scatter into the forest. Amid the chaos of exchanged gunfire, Beah escapes the rebels and believes himself alone until Junior and the others catch up with him. Reunited, the six boys make their way back to the village in which they had spent their time scavenging for food to sleep and consider their next steps.

Analysis

This chapter recounts Beah's first direct encounter with the rebels. The RUF members are portrayed as sadistic, violent young men entertained by the pain of others. When the rebels accuse the old man of failing to support their cause, Beah wonders "What cause?" He notices that whomever painted the initials "RUF" on all the walls of the village probably did not even know his alphabet. "Rather, he only knew what R, U, and F looked like" (p. 33). Beah considers the rebels to be ignorant young men enamored of killing and torture, not freedom fighters in the service of a greater cause.

The depth of Beah's love for his brother (and vice-versa) shows in the recruit selection scene. In both rounds, Beah and Junior are on the verge of being separated from one another. When he is told he will have to kill the weaker boys (and very likely watch his brother die), Junior cannot help but weep in anguish. But when the brothers find each other in the forest, Junior gives Beah "that smile he had held back when I was about to face death" (p. 36). Junior wants to reassure his younger brother, just as he has done in the past, but in the midst of an upheaval that has overturned their whole world, even the protective Junior is at a loss to care for his younger brother.

Summary and Analysis of Chapter 6

Summary

Despite the fact that a group of six boys is drawing attention from and instilling fear in the locals, Beah and his companions stay together out of a desperate need to feel safe. The boys decide to avoid the villages so as not to alarm the inhabitants, but as they leave the forested area at one point, they are accosted by a nearby village's machete-wielding guards. The guards take the boys to the village, where they are accused of being rebels. The entire village seems prepared to execute the boys as rebels when the village chief discovers Beah's rap tape. When it is played and the chief hears the strange music, he inquires where Beah got it. Beah explains what rap music is and that he and his friends had a dance group in Mattru Jong. At the mention of Mattru Jong, the chief asks if anyone present has spent time in Mattru Jong and can corroborate the boys' story. A young man steps forward and, calling Beah and his friends by name, saves their lives. Beah notes that he does not recognize the young man.

The villagers then give the boys cassava and smoked fish to eat and offer to let the boys remain with them. The boys are grateful, but choose to move on as they know the rebels will eventually reach this village as well. As they leave, Beah notices that his brother Junior has become unusually quiet.

Beah remembers when Junior taught him to skip a stone on the river. In the process, Beah fell and Junior got him to his feet and asked him if he were fine. As Beah in the present sits on the verandah of an abandoned house, he wishes Junior would again ask him if he were fine.

A group of travelers pass through the abandoned village, among them a woman who knows Gibrilla. She gives Gibrilla news of his aunt's whereabouts. The boys then head in that direction.

Gibirlla's aunt lives in Kamator. When the boys arrive, they are offered food and a place to sleep in exchange for acting as the village's watchmen. The boys accept and guard the village vigilantly for a month, after which time their wariness dims. Without the immediate threat of rebel invasion, the villagers decide that the boys need to work at farming to earn their keep. Beah learns how hard it is to farm as they are barely able to perform a portion of the work that the local villagers can accomplish.

When he sees a little boy who always starts fights in the village, Beah is reminded of his younger self and Junior, who were treated as outsiders in their own community due to their mother's departure. The adults' pity so angered Beah that he would sometimes kick their children at school.

A later attack on Kamator separates Beah from Junior; the brothers never see on another again.

Analysis

Beah makes use of flashback and foreshadowing both in this chapter. He calls upon his memory of Junior's stone-skipping lesson to illustrate the love and care Junior showed him growing up. The older brother's protection and concern contrast with the present situation, in which Junior is lost in his own thoughts and unable to console or reassure his little brother.

Then Beah flashes back to his experience at harvest time, when Beah's grandmother had allowed him to pour wine on the soil to thank their gods for a good harvest. This delicately-performed ceremony contrasts with Beah's current difficulties in performing the labor of the harvest.

Finally, Beah is reminded of his youth when he takes note of the little boy who always seems to start fights. This is the first time Beah has hinted that he was a troubled child, although the explanation that his mother's absence made him a "misfit" in his village is no surprise, as the reader already knows that Beah's parents are divorced and live in different villages.

At the end of the chapter, Beah foreshadows the tragedy of Junior's separation during a rebel attack on Kamator. He complains that all his (and the villagers') labor was for nothing, because "in the end, it all went to ruin, because the rebels did eventually come and everyone ran away" (p. 43). He ends the chapter stating "It was the last time I saw Junior, my older brother" (p. 43).

Summary and Analysis of Chapter 7

Summary

The rebels attack Kamator, surprising everyone in the village. They go so far as to take the village imam hostage and demand he tell them where in the forest the other villagers are hiding. The imam refuses to answer and is bound and burned to death by the rebels. His body is left in the village square as a warning. Beah escapes into the forest at the first sign of attack. He manages to find Kaloko, but loses Junior in the chaos. Kaloko and Beah return to the village after the attack, but can find none of their friends. The two boys find a family they know and stay with them for two weeks, all the while still unable to find Junior or their friends. Beah reflects on a time earlier in his life, when his father blessed the family's new home in Mogbwemo. His blessing included a prayer that the family would always stay together; to this prayer a village elder added that they would always be together, because even the dead lived on in the spirit realm. At this memory, Beah begins to weep for his lost family and friends.

For the next few weeks, Beah and Kaloko venture into Kamator every three days to see if anyone has returned to the village; all they see is emptiness and the vulture-picked corpse of the imam. Beah tires of living in fear and decides to head further away to find someplace safe from the RUF. Kaloko is too frightened to leave with him, so Beah sets out on his own. As he leaves the area he finds himself suddenly sorrowful to be totally alone for the first time since the rebel attacks on Mattru Jong. For five days Beah walks alone with no human contact. He sees some animals and learns through trial and error how to gather food to sustain himself. On the sixth day of his sojourn, Beah finds a group of eight people - four boys, two girls, and a man and woman - and approaches them carefully. He addresses the man in both the dialects of Krio and Mende, but receives no response. To his specific request for directions to Bonthe, an island rumored to be safe from the RUF, Beah receives a response from the man in Krio. The man gives him directions, but makes it clear from his face and posture that he wants Beah to move along. Beah continues on his journey.

Analysis

Beah describes the insidious influence of the RUF on civilians throughout the civil war zone. A twelve year old boy, alone or in a group, is a potential threat to others because he might be an RUF recruit. There is little Beah can do to convince this family otherwise, so he must continue on his way alone. Although Beah has noted the hospitality of villagers in other chapters, here he points out the fear and paranoia that grips those who have lost homes or loved ones to the rebels.

Again Beah uses a flashback to bring poignancy to narrative. At the moment he loses his last connection to his immediate family - his older brother Junior - Beah remembers his father's earlier dedication and blessing of their family home in Mogbwemo. Beah has already informed the reader that his father and mother are divorced, splitting Beah's life between their two homes (Mogbwemo and Mattru Jong); now the rebels have taken his father, his extended family, and his brother in succession, leaving him alone in the world. There is bitter irony in his father's prayer that the family "will always be together" (p. 47) and cold comfort in the village elder's prayer that they remain together "even in the spirit world" (p. 47). Beah confronts the fact that his best hope for reunion with Junior is in death.

Summary and Analysis of Chapter 8

Summary

Beah recounts his walking for two days without sleep, stopping only to drink water from streams. He cannot shake the feeling of being followed, and so he keeps pushing himself onward. On the third day, he becomes lost in a forest and has difficulty finding his bearings. He makes eye contact with a snake, which leads him to grab a stick for protection. Even after spending time familiarizing himself with his immediate vicinity, Beah is unable to gain a sense of direction. He resolves to make his temporary stay in this unknown location as comfortable as possible; he clears away dead leaves and marks his path from the campsite to the stream. There is enough food and water nearby that he can stay here indefinitely, so Beah decides to take a break from his walking to rest.

While resting, Beah recalls his visit (with Junior) to Kabati. He recalls his grandfather's lore about local leaves and bark which could be used for various medicinal purposes. Among them is a special medicine that improves the brain's ability to recall information; Beah remembers his grandfather giving this to him and claims it has given him a photographic memory to this day.

Beah decides to take a bath; lacking soap, he calls upon his grandfather's lessons and finds a particular kind of grass that provide a foamy substitute. Beah also washes his clothes and dries them during the day.

The loneliness of being in the forest affects Beah the most. Alone with only his constant thoughts, he cannot stop his mind from pondering the fates of his friends and family. He develops a fear of sleeping, anxious that his suppressed negative thoughts would come through in his dreams. As the days pass, Beah keeps searching for a way out of the forest; his efforts are in vain, however, for the forest seems to become thicker and more threatening no matter how far or in which direction he walks.

One evening Beah encounters a herd of wild pigs. He climbs into a tree to avoid them. However, when he climbs down - thinking them gone - he is attacked by two of the herd. Beah runs and narrowly escapes by climbing a tree. The pigs summon the rest of the herd and begin charging the tree to make Beah fall, but eventually give up as night falls.

Beah recounts a story his grandmother once told: there was a hunter of wild pigs who used magic to transform himself into a wild boar. He would lead the herd into an open area then transform himself into a human and shoot the pigs. The pigs discover the secret plant which the hunter is using to effect the transformation back into a human being; once he is gone, the pigs destroy every leaf of this plant they can find. When the hunter attempts his trickery, he cannot turn into a human again; the rest of the pigs surround and kill him. Now wild pigs distrust humans, fearing that any human being they see is there to avenge the hunter.

With the immediate threat of the pigs gone, Beah climbs down from his tree to continue walking. He remembers how his grandfather inserted medicine into his skin to protect him from snakebite and enable him to control snakes; however, when he was older Beah stopped believing in the medicine and lost his ability to stop snakes.

After more than a month of lonely wandering, Beah finally encounters people again. Among them are three boys - Alhaji, Musa, and Kanei - who had attended Centennial Secondary School with Beah in Mattru Jong. Three boys named Saidu, Jumah, and Moriba round out the group, which is on its way to the village Yele in Bonthe disctrict; they boys believe that village to be safe because they have heard it is occupied by the Sierra Leone Armed Forces. Despite the fact that the number of boys traveling together will cause problems, Beah remains with them because he does not want to be alone anymore.

Six days' travel later, the boys encounter an old man who can barely walk. He has been abandoned by the rest of the villagers, who fled into the forest when they heard that "seven boys" were on their way to the village. Once the boys explain who they are and what they are doing, the old man asks them to stay a while and keep him company. The boys ask him his name, but he avoids the question in order to save a place in the boys' memories for other things. The old man gives the boys directions then sends them on their way. From the old man, Beah learns that someone has started a rumor about the "seven boys," a rumor which paints the boys to be more dangerous than they really are.

Analysis

Beah again employs the technique of flashback in order to fill in the details of his life before the rebels attacked Mattru Jong. The repeated delving into this memory also underscore the way his mind worked while he spent so much time isolated in the forest. He connects his encounter with the snake to his grandfather's medicine allowing him to resist snakebites (which Beah says will not work anymore due to his lack of faith in the medicine), and utilizes his grandfather's forest lore to bathe himself properly. Through these flashbacks, Beah demonstrates how his family's legacy works to keep him alive and relatively comfortable despite the dire circumstances he finds himself in.

Beah also recounts his father's words: "If you are alive, there is hope for a better day and something good to happen. If there is nothing good left in the destiny of a person, he or she will die." These words sustain Beah's motivation to press onward even though he has no idea where his walking will lead. Beah places this recollection just prior to his encounter with the six boys, foreshadowing that his coming across the boys is part of "something good" left to happen to him as he awaited his destiny. The meeting does indeed become fortuitous, for the boys become a surrogate family for one another as the weeks progress.

Beah's reflection on loneliness indicates another unseen aspect of the rebels' evil: they leave their living victims isolated as orphans and widows. Beah feels most forlorn as he travels without direction through the ever-thickening forest; the external world reflects his own inner struggle with loneliness and fear. He has no direction - both literally and figuratively - and it is because of the rebels' attacks on the villages that Beah, and other like him, find themselves outcasts.

Summary and Analysis of Chapter 9

Summary

As Beah and his six companions travel through the forest, they hear an unfamiliar roaring sound. They immediately get off the road to hide, but the source of the noise does not change its proximity. Kanei finally decides to look toward the noise and discovers the source: the ocean. None of the boys had ever seen the sea before, so this scene of natural beauty gives them pause and a respite from their fears. They relax enough to dance and play soccer.

They continue down the beach to find a small village, but no inhabitants. All evidence points to a hurried and recent evacuation. Suddenly, a group of fishermen spring from their cover and seize the boys. The villagers have heard rumors that a young band of rebels are in the area, and accuse the boys of being hostile. After interrogating them, the fishermen take the boys' shoes and send them away.

Walking across the burning sand, the boys realize that their shoes were taken as a means of punishment. Despite the pain, they keep walking until sunset end eventually come upon an unoccupied hut. The boys take refuge in the hut and begin to treat their injured feet. The owner of the hut arrives, nearly leaves when he sees the boys, but remains when he notices their suffering. He stops Musa from pulling the grains of sand out of his blistered feet; instead, he offers them a treatment of steamed grass to ease their pain. For the next several days, their nameless host comes from his village to the hut in order to nurse them back to health with regular treatments and food. When Beah asks the man his name, the man replies that they need not share their names: "This way we will all be safe" (p. 63).

After a week of recovery, the man takes the boys to the ocean to soak their feet in the salt water. He has them soak their feet every day to promote healing and kill infection. The boys learn their caretaker is a member of the Sherbo tribe, and that he has not seen the violence of the war firsthand. At the end of the second week, an older woman enters the hut and urges the boys to leave. Beah can tell from her manner of speaking that she knew about the boys' presence in the hut all along. The boys flee, but are too late to escape the villagers who have learned of their presence.

Twelve men wrestle the boys to the ground and tie their hans, then bring them before their chief. The chief orders the boys stripped. Calling them "devils", the chief decides to drown the boys in the ocean. However, Beah's rap music cassettes are found. He explains he used to dance with his brother and friends before the war. The chief orders Beah to dance and he is convinced that the boys are not rebels, but lost children fleeing the violent conflict. When asked whether the boys had been assisted or had stayed in the fisherman's hut of their own accord, Beah tells the chief that the boys stayed there on their own to spare their caretaker from punishment. The chief releases them but orders them to leave the village and continue on their way.

Analysis

Beah notices that the natural beauty of the ocean can give succor to the weary, frightened boys: "My eyes widened, a smile forming on my face. Even in the middle of the madness there remained that true and natural beauty, and it took my mind away from my current situation as I marveled at this sight" (p. 59). The boys' chasing one another and playing soccer serves as a reminder that these are in fact children who have been exposed to the horrors of civil war. This poignant moment of play provides stark contrast to the terrors of previous chapters.

The cruelty of the fisherman reveals how far the terrorism of the RUF has spread; the boys, who are staying together for safety and emotional security, are rumored to be rebels and treated as hostile by nearly everyone they meet. Even on the sea shore, further than any of the boys have traveled, the fear of civil unrest makes the boys outcasts before they even meet anyone face to face.

In contrast, the lone fisherman shows them hospitality and kindness. Beah notes that he was ready to leave his hut to avoid them until he saw their wounds. The fisherman is moved to compassion for the boys and helps them to recover. He asks nothing in return, only asking that they do not learn his name. The boys return his kindness in the only way available - by not identifying him as an accomplice to their recuperation.

The difference between the reactions of the single man and the village provide the reader with insight into the character of the people of Sierra Leone. Taken on a case by case basis, the people are generous, kind-hearted, and sympathetic; however, when operating in a group mindset, with the safety of their entire village at stake, they become defensive, fearful, and - because of these two attitudes - sometimes cruel.

Summary and Analysis of Chapter 10

Summary

In the coming days, Beah and his companions encounter varying levels of hospitality at each of the villages they approach. Many are still afraid and hostile, but in some villages the boys are greeted kindly and offered food and rest. Beah finds these more pleasant experiences to be more wearying than ongoing fear and isolation. He says "I knew that it was temporary and that we were just passing through. It was much easier to be sad than to go back and forth between emotions" (p. 69).

At one village, the boys are invited to join a hunting party. They do so, and the hunt is successful; they return to the village with their game and a feast - complete with music and dancing - occurs that night. Even as they enjoy themselves, the boys realize that their happiness is only temporary. The next village they find is deserted, and appears to have been so for a long time. That night Musa tells the familiar story of Bra Spider, a trickster figure who usually ends up becoming the victim of his own clever plans. In Musa's story Bra Spider learns of several feasts happening on the same night; while everyone else gathers food and makes preparation for each feast, Bra Spider connives his way into an invitation to every one of the feasts. He puts one end of a rope in each village, tying the other end around his own waist, and leaves instructions for the villagers to pull on the rope when the food is ready. In this way, Bra Spider hopes to quickly arrive at each feast in succession and eat his fill. Unfortunately, the meals are all prepared around the same time, and Bra Spider finds himself pulled in all directions at once. This, Musa explains, is why spiders have thin waists. Although they all know the story, the boys enjoy Musa's retelling of it.

As he drifts off to sleep, Beah recalls his naming ceremony. Although too young at the time to actually remember the event, Beah has a vivid account of the ceremony from his grandmother. He remembers his grandmother's smile at the end of her telling him this story, then falls asleep.

The next morning the boys' supply of food is gone. They begin accusing each other of hoarding it, but Saidu puts a stop to the recriminations by pointing out that the bag is still tied but one of the corners has been chewed through. The boys track their nighttime thief and find a wild dog, ravenous with hunger. The boys chase the dog off but are unable to recover their lost food.

The boys keep walking, looking for food as they march. A crow falls from the sky and, despite some misgivings, the hungry boys cook and eat it. The next night, the boys' journey becomes eerie. The forest grows unnaturally silent. As they walk they see and hear three white-clad people ahead on the trail, so they hide in the bushes until the three figures pass. They can make out two tall forms and one smaller one, each with a cloth under its arm. The three figures seem to sense the boys' presence nearby and talk amongst themselves in voiced difficult to understand. The figures continue on their walk and the boys slowly creep out of the bushes. Saidu is rendered catatonic by the experience and must be carried until they cross the nearby bridge, at which point he comes to, coughs up blood, and proclaims the three figures to be ghosts. The other boys agree.

The next day the boys arrive at a large village in the midst of dinner preparations. One woman among the villagers claims to know Beah (although he does not recognize her) and gives him news that his brother Junior came through this village looking for him, and she has seen his mother, father, and younger brother as well. She tells him they headed to the neighboring village, which houses many refugees from Mattru Jong and Sierra Ritule mining district. Despite Beah's desire to set off immediately for the other village, the boys spend the night here to rest and relax. The boys sleep on the verandah of one of the houses, but that next morning Saidu does not wake up. The owner of the house comes out to help. He tries to wake Saidu, but concludes that the boy is dead. The village holds a funeral for Saidu, but there is difficulty getting it underway at first since none of the other boys is related to him. Kanei knows Saidu's family, so he stands in for them at the funeral. The boys are assured by the villagers that they have a place to belong to now, and they will always know where their friend is buried. Beah accepts their kindness while hiding the bitter sense that they boys have no control over their futures, and so have little chance of ever returning to their friend's gravesite.

Analysis

As with Chapter 9, this chapter mixes pleasure and pain for the boys. Beah narrates events which, while positive in the remembering, bring with them emotional pain at the longing they produce. Musa's story distracts the boys for a time, and even sends Beah into reverie about his grandmother, but the fact that these pleasant circumstances are memory and not reality is not lost on the boys.

The village they encounter is also a mixture of joy and despair. The villagers welcome the boys, and Beah receives hopeful news about his family. However, they lose Saidu in that village, which is yet another testament to the fact that any happiness they experience must be short-lived. Beah's reaction to the villager's hospitality - reminding them that their friend will always be buried here and therefore they have a place to return to - shows how the boys' harsh circumstances have hardened them to emotional happiness. He knows they have become survivors, not merely wanderers, and so will act first for self-preservation even above the comforts of friends and family.

Summary and Analysis of Chapter 11

Summary

The boys experience delayed grief for Saidu's passing. As they take a break from walking, Moriba begins to weep, followed by all the other boys save Beah. After a few minutes the boys stop their crying and continue their walk. From there on, the boys attempt to keep their hopes up. Alhaji hopes to see his mother in the next village, while Kanei believes they will at least find news of their families there.

As they continue, the sky grows dark and a heavy rain falls. The rain continues through the night, forcing the boys to remain in one place for the duration. The next morning they attempt to dry their wet clothes before continuing on their way.

As they get nearer to the village, the see a man cutting down ripe bananas. Beah recognizes him as Gasemu, one of the "notorious single men" of Mattru Jong. Gasemu studies the boys for a moment, then asks them to help him carry bananas to the village. As they gather the bananas, Gasemu indicates that he recognizes Beah and tells the young man that his family has been looking for him. At this news, Beah becomes impatient to reach the village but Gasemu insists on keeping a slow, steady pace. Beah becomes angry when Gasemu calls for a rest, but then Beah starts his walk before everyone else so that he may be in the lead.

Drawing nearer to the village, the boys hear gunshots, dogs barking, and people screaming. As they top the hill overlooking the village, they see smoke rising from the houses. They take cover in nearby bushes and listen to the gunfire and the screams of men, women, and children. Eventually the gunshots die down and Beah heads into the village to find his family. He finds many burnt-out houses and some charred corpses, but no one he can recognize as a member of his family. The boys hear screams coming from a burning building and break open the locked door, but only a woman and child escape the inferno.

Meanwhile, Gasemu has wandered to another part of the village. Here he sees the bodies of over twenty people, all shot in the back, and begins screaming and crying. Gasemu indicates to Beah the house his family had been staying in; Beah approaches the burnt-out hut and begins kicking its walls in rage and shock. The other boys are forced to pull him away.

Once he recovers from his undirected rage, Beah concludes that if Gasemu had not delayed them, he would have seen his family. He attacks Gasemu, eventually striking him with a pestle. The other boys hold Beah back again; Beah's anger infects them and they turn on one another, some blaming Gasemu for their not rejoining their parents, while others defend Gasemu as innocent of any intentional harm. Gasemu intervenes to stop the fighting, insisiting that "None of this is anyone's fault."

Further strife is prevented by the arrival of more than ten rebels in the village. Beah notes that only two of them look older than him. They rebels are congratulating each other on their destruction of the village, claiming that this is their most successful attack to date because none of the villagers escaped. While the rebels brag to one another and fire their guns randomly in the air, the boys and Gasemu hide and watch in anger and terror. One of the boys accidentally makes noise, drawing the rebels' attention. As if on cue, the boys and Gasemu bolt into the forest to escape. The rebels give chase into the night, only giving up once the moon sets and a heavy rain falls, obscuring their prey's trail. Once they lose their pursuers, Gasemu falls to the ground and begins sobbing. Beah feels frightened at the sight of a grown man crying. The boys pick Gasemu up and discover that he had been shot in the leg and side by the rebels during their chase. The boys try to stanch the flow of blood while Gasemu gives them directions to a wahlee (coffee processing place) and shows them the right path to take through the forest. Past midday, Gasemu asks to be set down on the ground; he falls prone and dies. The boys carry Gasemu's body to the wahlee and lay him at rest.

Analysis

Beah uses figurative language to contrast the beauty of nature to the boys' dire flight from the hostile rebels. He says the "kept running until the sky swallowed the sun and gave birth to the moon" (pp. 97-98) then "The moon disappeared and took the stars with it, making the sky weep" (p. 98). As with his prior uses of imagery and figurative language, Beah is emphasizing the natural beauty of Sierra Leone in contrast to the ugly brutality of the rebels and their victims. The repetition of the moon image from earlier chapters draws the reader back to that motif's meaning: there are some constants in the midst of chaos, even though they seem far away at the moment. The boys are running for their lives; nature seems to help them escape the evil the rebels intend for them by bringing rain to save them.

Beah also heightens the tension in this episode leading up to the village. His increased impatience with Gasemu's slow pace to the village hints that something dire may be on the other side of the hill. Gasemu's nonchalant attitude provides a stark contrast to Beah's hunger to see his family again after so long a separation. When the attack on the village is discovered, the reader automatically sympathizes with Beah's frustration, anger, and sense of sorrow when he blames Gasemu for his not being able to see his family again. Only when logical thought takes over does the reader realize that, had Beah made it to the village earlier, he would likely be among the charred or shot casualties they boys find in the village after the attack. From this we infer that Gasemu's slowness actually saved Beah's life.

Beah's feelings toward Gasemu reach their full development when the older man dies. He regrets having hit Gasemu with the pestle, and reflects that the (literal) blood on his hands from that conflict still remains even though Gasemu has spilled so much more blood since then. The boys do not abandon Gasemu's body, showing they have learned to honor the dead just as the previous village honored Saidu's passing.

Summary and Analysis of Chapter 12

Summary

The boys walk for several days, then are accosted by armed soldiers. The soldiers bring the boys back to Yele, a village occupied by government soldiers. Both soldiers and civilians live in the village and appear to be having a safe, almost happy life. Only the sight orphans - children whose parents were slain by rebels - dims the mood of the village. The boys begin assisting in daily work routines and believe they have finally found a safe haven. Beah's nightmares and migraines increase in intensity to the point of debilitating him from time to time, but he makes no mention of it to the village doctor.

One day, Beah notices the atmosphere of the village becomes tense. Lieutenant Jabati calls his soldiers to order and exhorts them for several hours. Later, Beah is caught looking at Lieutenant Jabati, who calls him to him. Jabati briefly discusses the book he is reading, Julius Caesar, then goes off into a reverie of his own. Beah leaves, mystified.

That night, the soldiers leave to confront the rebels. The next morning, significantly fewer soldiers return to the village. After several days of these skirmishes, the lieutenant gathers everyone in the village to the central square. There he informs them that the rebels are near and the military needs the help of able-bodied men or boys. He says those unwilling to join the military are free to leave, but they will have no more food or supplies from the village. The boys discuss their options and realize they only have one choice: join the Sierra Leonean army. To leave the village is to die.

The next day the lieutenant shows the villagers the mutilated bodies of a boy and a man. He informs the villagers that the two attempted to leave the village freely, but the rebels captured, tortured, and killed them. The lieutenant insists that this behavior shows the evil of the rebels and the need for good people to stand up against them.

Girls and women are sent to help in the kitchen, while boys and men are sent to the ammunition depot. Beah receives his weapon, an AK-47, and trembles with fear the entire time he holds it. The soldier distributing weapons encourages the new recruits that they will soon learn how to use this weapon to kill rebels. That night, Beah notices first that his former traveling companions have no desire to speak with one another (they are in different tents) and second that he is awake without a migraine for the first time in weeks.

The next morning the boys are summoned from their tents early to report for training. Beah helps his tent-mates to get out of bed and get into file. They exchange their old clothes for new shoes, army shorts, and t-shirts; in the process, Beah's precious rap tapes are thrown in the fire with his old shorts and destroyed. Beah learns that his tent-mates, Sheku and Josiah, emulate him rather than their commanding officer since they see him as an older brother figure. Their young commander, Corporal Gadafi, puts them through their paces practicing running, crawling silently, and recognizing hand signals so that they will not give away their positions in the forest by speaking. He rushes them through their breakfast in order to train them to eat within a minute, then teaches them how to fire, reload, and clean their AK-47s. Later Corporal Gadafi trains the boys to stab their enemies by practicing on a banana tree. The boys stab weakly at first, but improve dramatically when Gadafi tells them to remember that the rebel they may be attacking has done much worse to their parents. That night before bed, Beah reflects that he has learned the underlying lesson - that rebels were evil and deserved to die - quickly and well.

Analysis

In this chapter Beah describes the gradual indoctrination of young boys into the ways of warfare. The haven they have been led to becomes the training ground for their martial skills. Both Lieutenant Jabati and Corporal Gadafi use emotional arguments - the desire for revenge and fear of a cruel, inhuman enemy - to motivate the villagers to remain and support the military. His display of the corpses is an interesting parallel to the scene from Julius Caesar in which Mark Antony shows the commoners Caesar's assassinated body; Beah foreshadowed this connection when he describes Lieutenant Jabati's love of Julius Caesar prior to this moment.

Beah also uses foreshadowing to alert the reader that Yele, for all its seeming placidity and security, is a danger to the boys in ways they cannot foresee. He says "there were no indications that our childhood was threatened, much less that we would be robbed of it" (p. 101). This statement hints at the later induction into the military through emotional manipulation.

Beah also includes further flashbacks in this chapter to heighten the poignancy of the events which occur there. When he sees the soldiers and civilians playing soccer, he is reminded of his own time in a soccer league; he and his brother Junior were on the same team, and his parents were together in cheering them on. This memory brings with it a strong feeling of joy in Beah, who wants "to hold the moment longer, not only to celebrate our victory, but because the smile on my parents' faces that evening made me so happy that I felt every nerve in my body had awoken and swayed to the gentlest wind that sailed within me" (p. 102). This memory, juxtaposed with the words of Lieutenant Jabati and Corporal Gadafi later, gives Beah the anger he needs to turn his pain into hatred of the rebels and become a more effective soldier.

The scene in which Beah loses his rap tapes in the fire becomes symbolic when considered in light of what he is about to do. The rap tapes are representative of his childhood and happier days; they are destroyed in fire as Beah joins the military and begins his training to become a killer. As he has noted before, his childhood is destroyed.

Summary and Analysis of Chapter 13

Summary

A Sunday morning begins ominously as the lieutenant tells the new recruits to "worship your Lord today, because you might not have another chance." Most of the boys believe they are preparing for further drills, but Beah notices the adult soldiers gathering ammunition and supplies as well, and deduces that they are headed out to encounter the enemy. The corporal sets the boys and men in file and tells them to shoot anyone they see who is not wearing either a green head tie or a helmet like his own. Sheku, one of Beah's tent-mates, gathers too much ammunition and falls over, necessitating the lessening of his burden by the corporal. Then white capsules of an unknown drug are distributed to the young soldiers, allegedly to boost their energy. The soldiers, old and new, march out of the village toward their destination.

The company sets up an ambush in the forest and await the passing of rebels. Eventually they spot some people wandering through the forest; when it is clear that armed rebels are among the people, the Lieutenant Jabati gives the order and they open fire. Beah discovers that his trigger finger is numb and he cannot fire his weapon. Beah's other tent-mate, Josiah, is knocked onto a tree trunk by an RPG shell, breaking his back. Beah also sees Musa, dead from a head wound. At this moment, Beah manages to fire his G3 weapon and kill a man. He envisions the massacres he has seen the rebels perpetrate in the past, fueling his anger and bloodlust. He continues killing everyone he sees, stopping only to take ammunition, weapons, and supplies from their corpses.

The army returns to their village base at nightfall. While sleeping Beah has a nightmare that as he is picking Josiah up from the tree trunk, a gunman accosts him and points his rifle at Beah's head. Beah awakens from his nightmare firing his gun inside the tent, emptying the magazine. He notes that from that point on, he had no problem shooting his gun.

Analysis

The white capsules the young soldiers are given are probably some form of methamphetamine, since they are allegedly intended to boost the boys' energy. Beah notes later that he and the other soldiers become addicted to the drugs, just as they become dependent upon cocaine, brown brown, and marijuana. The need to deaden their senses to the slaughter around them is a recurring theme in this section of Beah's memoir; the drugs are the soldiers' coping mechanism against feeling anything of the horrors witnessed - and committed by themselves - during this conflict.

Beah's account of his first firefight demonstrates a young man's need to vilify his enemies in order to kill them. At first, Beah is unable to open fire on another human being even though he is ordered to do so. Only when his friend and tent-mate are killed does he realize the lives at stake and he is then able to open fire on the rebels. However, Beah overcompensates for his loss by killing any and every non-military person he sees and shutting off his emotions about the lives he is snuffing out. Once this monster of violence has been unleashed, he cannot control it or return to his prior state of pacific innocence.

The nightmare Beah experiences that night underscores the turning point for the young man in his shift from childhood to forced maturity. He has seen his friends die at the hands of rebels - up to this point, every offence the rebels committed in his sight had been against strangers - and now can unleash his pain and hatred on a visible target. From that point on, he has no difficulty identifying the rebels as inhuman enemies to be killed on sight.

Summary and Analysis of Chapter 14

Summary

Beah notices that his migraines lessen the more focused he is on "soldierly things." Along with the other boys and men, he becomes addicted to marijuana, *brown brown* (a mixture of cocaine and gunpowder), and the white capsules distributed by the officers. The drugs not only seem to give him energy, they also deaden his senses to the killings he commits. The soldiers spend their leisure time watching war movies such as *Rambo: First Blood* and *Commando*; from these films they take ideas they want to use on the battlefield.

Whenever supplies (including drugs) run low, the soldiers raid a rebel camp or, sometimes, a civilian village to get both supplies and more recruits. Beah's days become a haze of drug use and following orders with no clear plan given to the soldiers themselves. The violence quotient grows as the boys cheer their commanding officer for summarily executing a captured prisoner who refused to cooperate. Beah comes to see his weapon as his source of power and to rely on violence against rebels to give him a sense of purpose.

During a raid the army captures several prisoners; the younger soldiers, including Beah, are put in competition with one another to see who can kill his target by slitting his throat first. Beah connects the capture rebel to the deaths of his family members and wins the contest by killing his prisoner quickly. His achievement is celebrated by the other boys and adult soldiers as a milestone in his progress through military life.

Analysis

This short chapter offers much in the way of understanding Beah's life as a boy soldier. He concentrates a few years of violent military action into a few scenes, focusing here on the early rites of passage in his military career. The addiction to drugs, like so much else in the memoir, is offered as a matter-of-fact statement upon which the reader can render his/her own judgement; Beah only makes it clear that the addiction to the drugs is part of what helped the soldiers continue moving forward in their nightmare existence.

The incident of the killing contest works as a perverse coming of age moment for Beah. He takes a step from childhood into adulthood by murdering a defenseless man; he is only able to reconcile this with his conscience by first conjuring up the image of his murdered family and attributing their deaths to the rebel in front of him. The power of memory thus utilized is clear: by turning pain into hatred, Beah is able to kill the prisoner as smoothly as he might kill an animal, but the strength behind his blade is his anger and pain over the loss of his childhood.

Summary and Analysis of Chapter 15

Summary

It is now 1996 and Beah is 15. By now, Beah and his former companions are seasoned soldiers. With their squad, Beah, Alhaji, and Kanei travel to a nearby town of Bauya for ammunition. They know their friend Jumah is stationed there, and they look forward to talking to him; Beah also hopes to see Lieutenant Jabati again and discuss Shakespeare with his former commanding officer. After some joking about Jumah's increased strength (he can now carry a heavier weapon), the boys engage in their usual soldierly small talk, mostly about drugs. There is a social event in which the commanders mingle with everyone else; Beah feels that Lieutenant Jabati is a bit too jovial for the occasion. Beah learns that Corporal Gadafi is dead.

The next morning, Jumah and some other soldiers leave for their pre-arranged raid. A truck enters the village, discharging four men in UNICEF t-shirts. The boys are lined up and Lieutenant Jabati chooses fifteen of them, seemingly at random. Beah and his friend Alhaji are chosen, while Kanei is not. The chosen boys are ordered to turn in their weapons and equipment; Beah secretly disobeys the order by hiding his bayonet and a grenade in his clothing, then refusing to undergo a search by another soldier. The boys are loaded into the truck with several Military Police (MPs) - "city soldiers" whom Beah despises for their clean uniforms and weapons that belie no combat experience. Beah becomes increasingly anxious and angry at the seeming betrayal of his commanding officer.

After several hours, the boys are unloaded in Sierra Leone's capital city, Freetown. They are taken to a fenced compound and assigned beds. The UNICEF workers attempt to feed and clothe them, but the boys are uninterested in what the workers have to offer. Another group joins the boys and a fight breaks out as they attempt to learn whether each group has fought for the state or the RUF. Beah alters a hand-to-and fight to a standoff when he pulls out his grenade and threatens to throw it at the second group of boys unless they answer their questions. It turns out both groups are Sierra Leone military, so the boys become companions and the leader of the new group, Mambu, eventually becomes one of Beah's closest friends. In the meantime, the UNICEF workers, unfamiliar with the severity of the boys' military indoctrination, prove incapable of controlling their charges.

The united military boys head out to another group of boys sitting on the verandah. They want to know more about their situation and ask the boys if they know why their commanders gave them up to the civilians. The boys on the verandah refuse to answer, calling Beah's companions "civilians." Soon it comes out that the boys on the verandah are former RUF soldiers. This time a full-on fight breaks out. Beah throws his grenade at the rebels boys, but the explosion is delayed so it has little effect. Bayonets come out and boys begin slicing and stabbing one another. The MPs arrive to put a stop to the fight, only to be overpowered and have their weapons claimed by the opposing factions: one rifle for the RUF and one for the military. After a brief skirmish, six boys are dead (two of the military and four of the RUF). More MPs arrive to quell the fighting. The boys are separated and several are sent to Benin Home, a rehabilitation center on the outskirts of Freetown. As they are driven to Benin Home, Beah wonders what has become of his G3 weapon and what movie his squad might be watching that night. He shakes involuntarily as he goes through withdrawal from the drugs.

Analysis

This major turning point in Beah's life is complicated by his thorough dedication to the military by the time the UNICEF workers arrive. He is so loyal to his commanding officers, his squad, and his "cause" that being sent away to have a new life and an education seems like a betrayal to him. Beah does not say why he or the other boys were chosen - he suggests it was random. However, the fact that Alhaji was chosen while Kanei was not suggests that Lieutenant Jabati was choosing the youngest-looking of the boys who could feasibly have a second chance at a normal life. (Beah had previously noted that while Kanei was younger than Alhaji, Alhaji was often considered the younger of the two because Kanei was taller).

The boys' interactions with one another and their disdain for the UNICEF workers and the MPs brings to light the naivete of the UNICEF intervention in Sierra Leone. At this point, they believed the boys to be merely children who had been traumatized by violence. In the UNICEF compound it becomes clear that these young men are in fact deadly killers who cannot be cajoled into obedience when they are used to taking and giving orders in life-and-death situations. That the MPs are so ineffectual at keeping order suggests that Beah's experience in actual combat has matured him beyond their "pretend" militarism, making him the superior warrior.

The riots at the UNICEF compound also demonstrate how deeply-rooted the boys' military "brainwashing" (as Beah terms it) truly is. When offered a second chance at a civilian life after two years of combat, with new clothes, a safe place to sleep, and people who care for them, the boys turn the situation into a military endeavor. Strange boys, no matter their affiliation, are a threat until their motives and loyalties can be determined. The fight with the RUF boys accentuates how deep the ideological chasm is between boys who have suffered similar traumas, but been indoctrinated by opposite political factions.

Summary and Analysis of Chapter 16

Summary

Beah becomes frustrated at UNICEF's Benin Home. "It was infuriating to be told what to do by civilians," he says, adding "A few days earlier, we could have decided whether they would live or die." The dramatic contrast between his place in a military structure and his new life is irreconcilable. On the whole, the boys keep up an air of indifference to the medical and relief workers who attempt to care for them. They suffer drug withdrawals that lead them to steal medicine from the infirmary and reduce them to powder, but the drugs do not have the desired effect. The boys' violence is barely contained, sometimes spilling out into the neighborhood and often directed by the boys against one another.

The boys undertake a silent protest by dragging their mattresses outside each night to sleep in the open. Each day, the UNICEF workers return their mattresses to their bed frames; then the boys drag them outside again. One night it rains and the mattresses are left out in the sun to dry. When the boys ask why their mattresses are not on their beds, the workers respond that they must wait until the mattresses are dry to bring them in.

When the boys hurt the UNICEF workers, the workers respond by smiling patiently and continuing their relief efforts. This frustrates the boys, who want the civilian workers to respect (or fear) them as dangerous soldiers. Beah's migraines return with a vengeance. The boys decide to break the glass windows in the classrooms; Beah chooses to punch the windows with his fists and eventually manages to wound himself deeply enough to require a trip to the hospital. The nurse who treats him asks him his name, but Beah remains stubbornly silent. When he throws the glass of water she has given him across the room, shattering it, the nurse simply gives Beah a blanket and begins to sweep up the broken glass.

Later, Beah wakes up from his sleep to see a city soldier in the room with him and the nurse. Although he was sent to check up on Beah, the boy notices that the soldier is more interested in the nurse than in him. Beah contrasts this lieutenant with himself, a "junior lieutenant" in the Sierra Leone army. He recounts his experience in charge of a small strike force of boys. He and Alhaji emulate moves from the war movies they have watched as they attack a village. The squad kills everyone in the village, impractically leaving no one alive to carry supplies back to their base. Beah sends Kanei and Moriba back to base; the two boys return with the corporal, some soldiers, and several civilians to carry the supplies. Because of this raid, Alhaji acquires the nickname "Little Rambo." Lieutenant Jabati nicknames Beah "Green Snake" because he does not look dangerous, but he is deadly when he wants to be.

Returning to the present, Beah refuses to answer the city lieutenant's questions. Beah leaves the room and returns to the large hall where the boys gather for recreation. By now most of the boys have gone through their drug withdrawals, with the result that many were beginning to recall and face their wartime actions. The boys are told they will have classes for two hours each day; in class, the boys are disruptive and chaotic, learning little. They take their school supplies and sell them to outside vendors. Beah, Mambu, and Alhaji save their portion of the money for a trip to Freetown, which they undertake on the sly.

Freetown astounds Beah and Alhaji, who have never seen the city before. The boys enjoy it thoroughly, although they fall into their former military formation of Beah in front while Mambu and Alhaji walk behind. The boys return to the compound and tell the others of their adventure, prompting several unauthorized trips to the city. The UNICEF staff are forced to schedule regular trips to Freetown to prevent the boys' desertion, but tie participation in the trips to attendance in classes, thus finding a way to keep the boys in the compound and their classrooms.

Beah and the other boys become exasperated with the common refrain "It's not your fault." They abuse their teachers, medical workers, and other volunteers at the compound when they hear the statement. Many of the boys finally learn to sleep through the night, although they frequently awaken the next morning in the field with no memory of how they got there. Beah learns to sleep without medication, but at the same time finds himself facing his memories of the war. He recalls an incident where the prisoners from a raided village were buried alive. He recalls stabbing them in the legs and binding them so they could not flee. The boys forced them to dig their own graves then pushed them into them, then began shoveling dirt over them. Throughout the night the boy can hear the prisoners groaning and struggling for breath until they all die of suffocation. The boys joke about the prisoners already being buried. Around the campfire that night, Beah realizes he has several bruises from bullets that only barely missed killing him. He thinks has been too drugged and traumatized to realize the true danger of his experience.

Analysis

As in the previous chapter, Beah uses a flashback here to fill in the missing years between his induction into the Sierra Leone army and his transfer to the UNICEF compound. Whereas earlier flashbacks were of better times with his family (which he experienced them during times of intense trauma), now his flashbacks only go back to the war, even though he is experiencing them during a time of apparent security. He has truly lost his childhood to the war; now his memories only go back as far as his life as a soldier.

During one of the memories, Beah returns to his contrast between natural beauty and human ugliness. He recounts an encounter with rebels in which Moriba and others were killed. Though they have suffered losses, the soldiers press forward after the rebels to trail them to their base: "We fought all day in the rain," Beah writes. "The forest was wet and the rain washed the blood off the leaves as if cleansing the surface of the forest, but the dead bodies remained under the bushes and the blood that poured out of the bodies stayed on top of the soaked soil, as if the soil had refused to absorb any more blood for that day" (p. 150). The motif of nature as something beyond human good and evil, but which at the same time refuses to be sullied by the violence of men's battles, recurs here as a hint at Beah's own chance at redemption; if nature can cleanse itself of the blood of fallen soldiers, perhaps Beah and his fellow soldiers can do so as well.

Summary and Analysis of Chapter 17

Summary

The compound nurse begins to show a special interest in Beah, leading Alhaji to tease him that she "likes" him. Beah ponders her motives but cannot comprehend them. He becomes angry when she asks him his name (because he knows she knows it), but when he tells her his name she tells him her own: Esther. She expresses a desire to be his friend, but only if she can trust him. Throughout their subsequent visits, Esther turns the tables on Beah by making it seem that he needs to earn her trust rather than the other way around. Beah responds to her overtures, particularly when she buys him a Walkman cassette player and rap tapes. She keeps the player and tapes in her office so that the other boys will not attempt to take it from him, offering Beah an open invitation to come in to listen any time.

Beah eventually opens up to Esther and recounts his experience being ambushed by rebels in the forest. In the bloody firefight Beah is shot three times in the foot; he awakens to find the sergeant doctor treating him and doing all in his power to make sure Beah survives the injuries. Beah states that this is the moment he realized his loyalty to the military would stay strong. Once the doctor is able to remove the bullet lodged in Beah's foot, the boy begins recovering. Before he is fully mobile, he leaves his bed and asks for his weapon back. He gets it and fires off some practice rounds while bracing himself against a wall. Three weeks later rebels attack their base; they are repelled or killed, with a few captured and brought back to the base. Lieutenant Jabati identifies the captives as men responsible for the wounds to Beah's foot. Beah shoots them in their feet and watches them suffer all day before delivering mortal shots to their heads that night because he is tired of hearing them cry.

Beah surprises himself by opening up to Esther in this way; however, Esther responds with the common refrain, "None of what happened was your fault." This angers Beah, who feels that the "not your fault" line shows a lack of understanding of the boys' maturity. That night Beah attempts to recall his childhood, but all he can remember is the first time he slit a man's throat. He has a severe migraine that night and cannot sleep for fear of nightmares.

Analysis

In the UNICEF compound, Beah finally begins to trust someone. He had learned through hard experience that circumstances would collaborate to cause him harm; even in the military, where he learned comradeship through blood spilled, Beah found that he could be betrayed: "People like the lieutenant, whom I had obeyed and trusted, had made me question trusting anyone, especially adults" (p. 153). When even a man who held others' lives in his hands could turn traitor (by sending Beah with the UNICEF workers), there was no one left in Beah's world to confide in. He has learned that "people befriended only to exploit one another" (p. 153).

Esther manages to overcome this barrier through a combination of reverse psychology and patience. She challenges Beah to earn her trust, rather than offering to earn his; she also waits for him to be ready to talk, rather than insisting he answer her questions. Her knowledge of his pre-war interests (gleaned from the questionnaires the boys answered in class) allow her build a bridge to Beah - one which eventually allows him to speak plainly to her.

When he confides in Esther his terrible experience in taking vengeance upon the rebels who shot him in the foot, he is ostensibly giving her background for where his scars originated. However, what he is really doing is tearing down the wall he has erected to protect himself from harm. This one crack in the wall allows him to eventually speak much more openly and begin to feel the emotions he has long tried to suppress.

At one point, Beah attempts to remember his childhood. However, "it was impossible, as I began getting flashbacks of the first time I slit a man's throat" (p. 160). Beah's use of flashbacks throughout the preceding chapters has been building to this moment; his memories as a fugitive from the rebel onslaught are always of his childhood, of happier times and memories which keep him stable in an unstable world. Once he is inducted into the military - or as he puts it, once his childhood is destroyed - he no longer employs flashbacks to his youth. From this point on in the memoir, his flashbacks are all of bloody confrontations and violent fates met by both rebels and soldiers alike. The war has truly destroyed his childhood by denying him access even to the memories of his happier youth.

At the end of the chapter, Beah tells Esther "about the shapes I used to see in the moon when I was much younger" (p. 166). This breakthrough moment marks the return of his positive childhood memories (echoing the first flashback of hope from Chapter 1) and the beginning of his healing process. Esther's gift of a Walkman and rap tapes to replace those destroyed in the war also symbolize a new start. Perhaps Beah can rediscover and reclaim his childhood through her help.

Summary and Analysis of Chapter 18

Summary

Beah confesses to Esther that he feels he has nothing to live for, since his family is gone. She tells him to consider her his sister, which he agrees to so long as he adds the qualifier "temporary" to the title. When Esther laughs, it reminds Beah of a girl named Abigail, whom he had known briefly in secondary school. He wishes Abigail and Esther were the same person, so that they would have a shared past to connect them better.

Visitors from the European Commission, the UN, and UNICEF arrive the next day to meet the boys and look at the center. Mr. Kamara, the director of the center, greets the men and has the boys assembled to put on a talent show for the visitors. Beah reads a monologue from Julius Caesar and then performs a hip-hop play about a former child soldier that he has written himself. His performance at the talent show garners the attention of both the visitors and Mr. Kamara, who asks Beah to become the spokesperson for the center. While Beah belives Kamara is overstating the his charisma, he agrees. Two weeks later, he begins a series of presentations decrying the state of child soldiers, describing how it must be stopped, and encouraging his audiences that child soldiers can be rehabilitated - pointing to himself as an example.

Six months into his time at the center, Beah is surprised by the arrival of his childhood friend Mohamed. The boys quickly renew their friendship and begin to spend time together at the center from that point on.

The next month, Leslie arrives with the news that Beah has reached the point where he can be returned to normal society ("repatriated," as Leslie calls it) with a foster family. Since UNICEF cannot locate any of Beah's biological family, a foster family seems to be the only option. Beah recalls to Leslie an Uncle Tommy whom his father had sometimes spoken of, but whom he has never met. It happens that Uncle Tommy lives in the city. Leslie takes the information Beah has given him to continue his search, despite the fact that Beah is not optimistic that he will find a living relative.

Later, Leslie brings Beah's uncle to visit him at the center. The older man greets Beah with great affection and even begins to weep. Despite Beah's protest that he does not know the man, Uncle Tommy replies "...we cannot go back. but we can start from here. I am your family and that is enough for us to begin liking each other"(p. 172). Beah's uncle promises to visit every weekend and anticipates the day when Beah can return with him to his home to meet his aunt and their children. Beah is pleasantly surprised that his uncle keeps his word and visits every week; the two go on long walks and get to know one another.

One weekend, Uncle Tommy takes Beah to visit his wife and children. Beah's greets the boy as her "son," just as his uncle had, and introduces him to their children -

actually the children of family members whom the couple has raised as their own. Beah later learns that his grandfather had had many wives and that he has many more relatives than he had ever known about.

Analysis

Beah's fortunes take a turn toward improving greatly in this chapter. Beah notes his own reluctance to believe circumstances can improve (the unlikely possibility of Leslie finding his uncle) and his deeply-ingrained distrust of others (telling Tommy "I don't really know you"). Again persistence triumphs as Uncle Tommy keeps his word and visits Beah every week. Like Esther, Uncle Tommy does not push Beah to tell him about his experiences and continues to overwhelm the boy with affection and love.

On one of Beah's walks with Uncle Tommy, he has the opportunity to connect with the older man in a way he had previously wished to connect with Esther: by bringing up one of his father's few accounts of his childhood with Beah's uncle, the boy is able to draw the older man out and discuss a shared history. Although his own childhood is still a tender subject, Beah is able to enjoy his uncle's memory of a childhood that took place a generation ago. This also helps Beah to feel a connection to his missing family.

Summary and Analysis of Chapter 19

Summary

Beah eventually leaves to stay permanently with his uncle. Before he leaves, he says goodbye to Esther, who gives him her address so he can visit. He visits once, but finds her on her way to work; it is the last time he sees her. Beah bids a tearful and heartfelt farewell to his friends at Benin Home, then leaves to join his new family.

Beah arrives in his new home and is treated to a feast prepared by Aunt Sallay. Allie, the oldest of his new "siblings" shows Beah around and tells him where he will sleep. Beah quickly assimilates to the ways of the family, although he is unable to speak frankly about his time in the military. Allie takes Beah dancing; Beah meets a girl whom he later begins dating, but the relationship does not develop because Beah cannot find words to express his days as a child soldier.

Later, Leslie comes to see Beah at his uncle's house. He brings with him an invitation from Mr. Kamara to interview for one of two positions to travel to New York to speak to the United Nations about the situation in Sierra Leone. Beah agrees to the interview, but his uncle half-heartedly warns him not to get his hopes up. At the interview, Beah finds himself set apart from all the city boys who dress nicely and understand urban fixtures such as an elevator. The other boys laugh at Beah's naivete. However, when he is interviewed Beah tells his examiner that he is more qualified to speak to the UN because he has experienced child soldiering and rebel atrocities firsthand, whereas these other boys have only heard or read about it. The interviewer smiles at Beah, leading the boy to think the man is not taking him seriously. Nonetheless, Beah is called back to begin the process of preparing for his trip to the United States.

Throughout the arduous preparation to leave, Beah's uncle jokingly warns Beah again not to get his hopes up. Even on the day Beah departs for the airport to fly to the U.S., his uncle and the rest of his new family laugh and joke that he will only be "late for dinner."

Analysis

Beah captures the whirlwind nature of his changing circumstances through abrupt shifts in setting and time in this chapter. In a matter of pages, Beah is dining at his new home, then dancing at a pub, then interviewing in a tall building in the city. Not much later he is at the Sierra Leone embassy and back at his temporary home packing his bags to fly to America.

An ironic contrast in naivete is present in this chapter. Whereas Beah is unfamiliar with urban living conditions (as displayed in his confusion at the nature and operation of an elevator), the boys with whom he is competing are unaware of the harsh realities Beah has grown up dealing with every day. Beah's interchange with the CAW interviewer, in which he takes the interviewer's smiling as a sign that he thinks Beah's suffering is humorous, presages the later encounter at the Sierra Leone embassy, where the round-faced interviewer on the other side of the glass demands documents proving Beah was born in Sierra Leone: "I became really upset and almost slapped the man…He was naïve about the reality I was trying to explain to him" (p. 189). Beah has fought and killed men over political ideology and in order to survive; this government bureaucrat considers himself to possess power because he can demand a piece of paper that was most likely destroyed by the very violence that created Beah's situation. Despite his seemingly uncouth nature, Beah is most qualified to speak at the UN.

Summary and Analysis of Chapter 20

Summary

Arriving in New York City, Beah is immediately struck by the dissonance between his rap-music-informed view of the city and what he sees before him. Among the unexpected sights are the many people walking the streets (Beah had imagined everyone driving sports cars). Seeing New York winter for the first time, Beah is amazed and daunted by the extreme cold and learns the word "snow."

Beah, his traveling companion Bah, and their sponsor Dr. Tamba check into the hotel to stay for the duration of the conference. The morning of the United Nations First International Children's Parliament, Beah meets 56 other children from 23 different countries, all here to speak before the United Nations. All of the children have difficult lives in common, regardless of where they hail from. Beah connects with a facilitator named Laura Simms, a storyteller who holds a workshop to help the children tell their stories in a more compelling way. Beah is impressed to find a storyteller here in America, so far from his own story-centered culture in Sierra Leone. Laura also procures winter jackets for Beah and Bah, who only have their lightweight African clothing to wear.

Each day the children and facilitators gather to discuss their lives, but also to develop solutions to the problems of their various countries. Each discussion leaves the children hopeful that they can transform their suffering into happiness by making their lives known to the world. On the second night after the conference, Beah and Madoka from Malawi accidentally walk into Times Square. Beah is overcome by the displays everywhere and the glittering buildings.

On the last day of the conference, a child from each country speaks at the UN Economic and Social Council chamber about their experiences. Beah decides to eschew the speech written for him in Freetown in favor of speaking from his heart. He relates his trials and travails and ends by rejecting his identity as a soldier and insisting that taking revenge only perpetuates the cycle of violence. After the presentations, all the children sing a chant they had written together, followed by other songs. Everyone is moved by their sense of unity as well as the knowledge that they are not returning to peaceful homes.

The next evening, Laura accompanies Beah, Bah, and Dr. Tamba to the airport for their return flight to Sierra Leone. By the end of the car ride, everyone but Dr. Tamba is in tears from sorrow over their imminent parting. Laura gives Beah her address and phone number in order to keep in touch. The Sierra Leoneans board the plane and head back home. Beah is days away from his sixteenth birthday.

Analysis

Beah emphasizes the difference of the world he enters in New York City. Not only the environment and the people, but also the sense of security and love which contrast sharply with Beah's life in Sierra Leone. Meeting other children who have suffered as well give Beah a sense of belonging that he has missed for so much of his life. He sees that innocence, suffering, and hope transcend political or geographical borders.

Beah telegraphs his future in a flash forward involving Laura Simms: "When she became my mother years later, ashe and I would always talk about whether it was destined or coincidental that I came from a very storytelling-oreinted culture to live with a mother in New York who is a storyteller" (p. 197). Having passed through the worst of his suffering in the memoir, Beah is ready to give the reader hope for Beah himself, to remind us that there is a "happy ending" of sorts. That Beah and his adoptive mother Laura would discuss destiny or coincidence leaves the question open for the reader to ponder as well - was Beah drawn to Laura because of their common bond of storytelling, or is this merely a happy accident? And in the greater scope, is it Laura's support and eventual adoption of Beah that provides him the opportunity to create this very memoir, so rich in narrative appeal, to recount the horrors and hopes of child soldiers in Sierra Leone?

Summary and Analysis of Chapter 21

Summary

Beah returns home and attempts to resume a normal life. His long-time friend Mohamed now lives with Uncle Tommy's family. The boys start school again at St. Edwards' Secondary School; Beah is excited to resume his formal schooling. However, Mohamed and Beah are shunned at school on their first day because their past as soldiers has been discovered by the other students, who now fear them.

On the morning of May 25, 1997, Beah hears the sound of gunshots near the State House and House of Parliament buildings. He and Mohamed immediately fear that all they have suffered is about to repeat itself. The central prison is opened and the prisoners freed to loot and commit violence throughout the city. Some look for revenge against the judges and lawyers who imprisoned them, while others join the soliders, who are doing most of the looting. Johnny Paul Koroma comes on the radio, announcing himself as the new president of Sierra Leone. He is head of the Armed Forces Revolutionary Council, a body whose main purpose was to overthrow the democratically elected President Yejan Kabbah. Later that night the radio informs the people that the RUF and military have joined forces to oust the civilian government. A state of martial law results.

Beah and Mohamed make their way to a secret market to get food and supplies for their family. The market is chaotic, full of desperate people, but the two boys manage to get the items they came for. As they are leaving, a Land Rover full of armed men drives into the market. They fire a warning shot and order everyone to put down their food. A woman panics and is shot in the head. Beah and Mohamed grab their supplies and sneak away. While escaping, they pass some protestors and then a group of armed men following the protesters and civilians, firing their weapons and throwing tear gas. The two boys make their way to a gutter to hide until nightfall.

When the boys arrive home, they find Uncle Tommy on the verandah, tears in his eyes. He embraces the boys and tells them never to go back to the city, but they protest that they will have to when the supplies run low again. The violence lasts another five months, heralded by the constant sound of gunfire from the city. A neighbor who lives a few doors down, along with his wife and two sons, are pulled from his home, shot, and their bodies thrown into a gutter. During this time, Beah has lost contact with Laura Simms in New York.

Uncle Tommy becomes sick and eventually dies of a fever. They bury him the next morning while Beah's cousins ask who will take care of them now. A few days later, Beah is able to make a collect call to Larua Simms. He asks her if he can stay with her; she replies that he can, so Beah begins his dangerous trek to escape Sierra Leone.

A long, arduous journey ensues, during which Beah is forced to spend most of his saved money for bribes at checkpoints; he his sickened to see even civilian Sierra Leoneans take advantage of each other in this way. Immigration officers require the refugees pay money to cross the border out of sierra Leone into Guinea. Beah is able to make it across the border to Guinea, but there he encounters another difficulty: the national language of Guinea is French, which Beah does not speak. He manages to find someone who speaks Krio, and the two of them find a bus to get them closer to the Sierra Leonean embassy in Guinea, which has been opened as a temporary encampment for refugees. That night Beah listens to stories told by others and remembers one his grandfather told long ago:

A hunter goes into the bush to kill a monkey. Knowing he is a target, the monkey tells the hunter, "If you shoot me, your mother will die, and if you don't, your father will die." The hunter is left in this dilemma for the audience to discuss and attempt an answer. None of the children's answers are considered good enough by the storyteller, but Beah comes up with his own answer and rationale: "if I were the hunter, I would shoot the monkey so that it would no longer have the chance to put other hunters in the same predicament." With this statement, Beah ends his memoir.

Analysis

The violence in Freetown (and all over Sierra Leone) parallels and expands upon the violence Beah has already encountered throughout the first two thirds of the book. His sense of déjà vu is clear, as is his frustration at seeing the same evils perpetrated without being able to do anything about them: "I was afraid that if I stayed in Freetown any longer, I was going to end up being a soldier again or my former army friends would kill me if I refused" (p. 207). His prior experience does give him an advantage over the civilians in surviving the uprising, but that is small comfort to him as he is forced to flee yet again from a home that has become unsafe.

The loss of Uncle Tommy marks the moment Beah decides he must leave Sierra Leone for good. He knows he cannot care for his family, and he is afraid he will end up in the military, committing the atrocities he has been redeemed from, all over again. Only Laura Simms offers him a lifeline: a new home in New York City, far from the violence and political upheaval of his homeland.

The military coup brings to light the violent and selfish nature of the allegedly politically-motivated RUF and Armed Forces Revolutionary Council. They admit to overthrowing the democratically-elected government; they are also supported by the military, boys and men whom Beah once fought alongside against the RUF. Now the sides have become soldier versus civilian - no ideologies divide warriors against each other. Now it is every man for himself.

Beah again points out the effects of war on the children, this time in observing his younger cousins: "Children played guessing games, telling each other whether the gun fired was an AK-47, a G3, an RPG, or a machine gun" (p. 205). Childhood games have transformed into a competition to name the weapon of choice; innocence has once again been lost to violence.

The story Beah chooses to end the memoir with gives insight into Beah's attitude toward the oppressors in Sierra Leone. The tale of the hunter is meant as a childhood philosophical discussion to force young men and women to weigh an impossible dilemma. Beah knows his choice seems hard-hearted (resulting in his mother's death), but he wants to focus on solving the greater problem beyond the choice between the life of one parent or another. He identifies the monkey who forces the choice as the true threat, and wishes to eliminate that threat to future "hunters." From this the reader can infer that Beah would see the military regime in Sierra Leone toppled so that it no longer forced boys to choose between life and death, between family and military service, or between childhood and violence - even if it demands a sacrifice. Beah's childhood and innocence were sacrificed, but with this memoir, his words can expose and hopefully help end the atrocity.

Suggested Essay Questions

1. **How does isolating himself emotionally help Beah to survive his experiences in the Sierra Leone civil war?**

   Beah's experiences force him to deny his emotional side in order to survive. His flight from RUF attacks on the various villages in Sierra Leone requires him to let go of attachments to family and friends. Although he holds out hope to see his family, he has no choice but to close off himself to the world. Emotional attachment can be weakness, and weakness can get you killed. Even when he joins forces with groups of friends (first Talloi, Gibrilla, Kaloko, and Khalilou, and later, Kanei, Musa, Saidu, Jumah, and Moriba) Beah remains emotionally distant from his companions. When the boys bury Saidu, they know that they will never visit to his gravesite, despite the villager's efforts to comfort them with an open invitation to return. Over the months on the run, Beah gets separated - sometimes in death - from his companions. The unpredictability of his life dictates that he stay detached. Even after he has begun rehabilitation, he is only able to call Esther a "temporary" friend. He has been living too long with the goal only to remain alive for one more day.

   When he becomes a soldier, Beah's trainers use drugs and emotional manipulation - teaching the boys to picture their targets as the men who burned their villages and killed their families - to push the boys to acts of violence agains the rebels. Beah finds that he must suppress his emotional reaction to the atrocities he commits or lose his focus and, thereby, his life.
2. **How does Ishmael Beah address the loss of innocence in *A Long Way Gone*?**

   While Beah's memoir is written largely in a matter-of-fact tone, he does use several devices to illustrate the theme of loss of innocence: use of flashbacks, symbolism, and nature motifs.

   Beah states plainly that his induction into the Sierra Leone military at the age of 13 was the end of his childhood. Although the violent pursuit of rebels across Sierra Leone traumatized Beah, it is not until he is turned into a killer that he believes himself to have lost his innocence. At this point, Beah stops utilizing flashbacks to his childhood, clearly delineating his old "good" life with his new "bad" life. Before this point, his memories were comforting to him during his wandering and, narratively, they served the function of reminding the reader that Beah is still a child caught in an impossible situation.

   When he is at the Benin Home, he only starts to delve back into childhood memory/flashback when he is able to work through his war experiences.

The phantasmagoric nightmares serve as a barrier to remembrances of his family; only by moving through the war images is he able to call up his childhood memories, and then begin healing.

Beah's rap tapes also symbolize his innocence. His childhood ended without warning, when he and his friends were traveling to practice dance routines. The tapes remain with Beah throughout the months spent avoiding RUF attacks. They save his life - convincing the a chief that he is still a child at heart and not a "devil" - and narratively become a physical representation of his innocence. The tapes are burned when the army takes his cloths, thus continuing their symbolic importance. Music, a reminder of his old life, becomes a gateway to healing when Esther's gift of a Walkman helps Beah to open up at Benin Home.

Throughout the book, Beah notices and describes the natural world around him in beautiful detail. As the violence increases, the references to nature subside. The scene where Beah and his friends see the ocean for the first time - creating a much-needed respite - stands out as the strongest example. They play together, once more becoming children.

3. **How does Ishmael Beah use memory as a comfort in his most difficult circumstances?**

   Ishmael Beah refers to memories throughout A Long Way Gone, relayed as flashbacks. In difficult times, he clings to moments from happier years - especially those occurring before his parents' divorce. By focussing on such memories as stories his grandmother told him, his grandfather's medicines, and the blessing of his childhood home, Beah is able to find solace in madness. If he remembers a time when he was happy, there is hope that he can regain that life. He sometimes feels these memories are a burden, reminding him as they do of a time when his life was much better than his current circumstances. Still, he returns to memories of his family as a sign he has recuperated from his life of violence.

4. **Describe some of the tactics used by the military to indoctrinate child soldiers, and their lasting effects on Beah.**

   In order to acclimate children to war and mold them into effective killing machines, Lieutenant Jabati and his men employ several different tactics: drugs, pop culture, and several modes of emotional manipulation transform boys into killers. When Beah is about to go on his first raid, he is handed white pills for "energy". These white pills, plus *brown brown* and marijuana create a constant haze. Ultimately, there is a disconnect from reality when the addiction takes hold. Without the drugs, as in Benin Home, Beah becomes aggressive and the boys resort to raiding the hospital to quell their hunger. When the drugs begin to wear off, Beah's headaches return - as do images of slaughter.

Violent movies, like the drugs, help to create a surreal, dreamlike atmosphere for the boy soldiers. They would often go on attacks in the middle of films like *Rambo* or *Commando*, sometimes acting out techniques seen in the movies on the battlefield, and then pick up where they left off when returning to base. The reality of war bleeds into the fiction of war films, which helps to further disconnect the soldiers from the truth of situation. Beah's almost cinematic nightmares feel like a product of this conditioning and only through rehabilitation is he able to confront and discuss his wartime actions.

When he is being trained, Beah learns to channel his rage and seek vengeance for his family. Though he had spent months suppressing his emotions for the sake of survival, Lieutenant Jabati and his men encourage Beah and the boys to tap into the fear and anguish in order to kill. This gives the boys a personal motivation for each kill; though it is unlikely they are targeting the actual rebels who murdered their families. Jabati also exploits his authority by staging contests where the person who kills a prisoner fastest is the "winner". When Beah wins, there is a sense that Jabati is proud of him. In a way, Jabati becomes a father figure to the boys. When Beah and Alhaji are given up to the UNICEF workers, Beah feels betrayed by Jabati. In creating a power dynamic between them, Beah's trust is shattered. It takes the efforts of nurse Esther and other aid workers to begin rebuilding Beah's trust in adults.

5. **Discuss Beah's time in Benin Home. How did the boys' behavior change throughout their time in rehabilitation?**

When Beah and Alhaji are handed over to the UNICEF relief effort, they feel betrayed by Lieutenant Jabati. The boys are still in soldier mode when the arrive at Benin Home; when they meet other refugee children who were RUF, a fight ensues and people die. Beah and his friends are resistant to schooling and talking about their experiences. They are still in survival mode, unable to trust anyone and suffering through withdrawal from drugs. Beah and his friends take unauthorized trips to Freetown, and the staff has no choice but to start taking them into the city - but they also bribe the boys into remaining in class. This action - along with Esther's gift of a Walkman and rap tapes - is a moment where the aid workers show respect for the boys at Benin Home. Slowly but surely, with the help of their caretakers, the boys begin to open up about their time at war. When the drugs subside for Beah, his headaches return with a vengeance. It takes him a long time to be able to cope with his new surroundings, as he had gotten used to living without hope of a life on the other side of war.

6. **How do Beah's experiences in New York City change the course of his life?**

In Chapter 20, Beah travels to New York to speak at the UN. He finds the city is different than he expected, as he had envisioned people racing down the street in sports cars. Beah sees a world outside of violence and war - a world that is very different from Sierra Leone. He learns the word "snow" and repeatedly visits the dreamlike Times Square. Beah also finds that his story is sadly not unique. At the UN, he talks with many children who had similar experiences in their own countries. Beah realizes that he is not alone. Laura Simms, a storyteller who helps the children with their presentations, forges a deep connection with Beah; he eventually flees the war to live with her in New York. Other than laying the groundwork for a future home and life in the United States, the trip to New York gives Beah hope. At the end of the chapter, he is sad to leave, but also knows that if he dies in Sierra Leone, people will care. After years of witnessing and causing meaningless death, Beah comes to understand the value of his own life.

7. **Discuss Beah's writing style. How does writing from the perspective of a child help create an understanding of the child soldier experience?**

Though his memoir was written when he was 27, Beah adopts a writing style appropriate to his age during the events described. This helps the reader to gain insight into what it would be like to live through his experiences. Essentially, the reader is given only the information Beah himself would be privy to at 12 and 13. The villagers - especially the children - largely do not know the motivations and causes that the RUF are operating under; they are familiar only with the violence they inflict. Until it is at his doorstep, the war was something he heard rumors of but didn't fully comprehend; by denying the readers a historical and political context, we are thrust into his position and feel his confusion and fear when the rebels attack.

Throughout his trials, Beah uses memories of his childhood as a buffer to the harsh reality. These instances help remind the reader that he is still indeed a child, which illustrates the evils of the civil war. Also, Beah does not shy away from the grittier aspects of his experience, like the death of prisoners at his hand. He does not judge or interpret his or any one else's actions, instead letting the reader moralize on his or her own. By not ruminating or reflecting on the atrocities, the reader can truly get into Beah's head and experience the horrors alongside him.

Sierra Leone Civil War

The Sierra Leone civil war began in 1991 with the attacks of the
United Front (RUF), led by former army corporal Foday Sankoh,
military and civilian targets. While allegedly begun as a response
government of President Joseph Saidu Momoh, the RUF quickly
terror and violence with little regard to its ostensible political agenda. The RUF captured towns on the Liberian border, killing and torturing numerous citizens. The President is ousted in 1992, setting up a cycle of military coups for the next five years. In 1996, after the first multi-party election in nearly thirty years, Ahmad Tejan Kabbah is elected President. He signs a peace accord with the RUF. Kabbah is ousted by yet another military coup, led by Johnny Paul Koroma and the Armed Forces Revolutionary Council (AFRC) - a force consisting of both army and RUF soldiers who previously fought against one another.

Atrocities were committed on both sides of the conflict, which resulted in over 50,000 killed and one million people displaced. Despite the level of violence, national attention was not drawn to Sierra Leone until 1999, when the United Nations intervened to establish the Lome Peace Accord. This treaty made the RUF commander vice-president of the country with control over Sierra Leone's valuable diamond mines.

Despite the accord, RUF forces continued their attacks and seemingly random acts of violence against government and civilian targets. The UN sought disarmament, but response on both sides was slow. Eventually, Great Britain intervened, sending in troops to capture RUF forces and restore full power to then-president Kabbah. In 2000, RUF leader Sankoh was captured. Over the next year, UN forces complete disarmament and the war is declared over in 2002. Newly re-elected President Kabbah declared the conflict ended in 2002.

Sierra Leone Civil War Timeline (BBC News):
http://www.bbc.co.uk/news/world-africa-14094419

Author of ClassicNote and Sources

Todd Gordon, author of ClassicNote. Completed on October 31, 2011, copyright held by GradeSaver.

Updated and revised Christine McKeever July 30, 2012. Copyright held by GradeSaver.

Beah, Ishmael. A Long Way Gone. New York: Sarah Crichton Books, 2007.

"Global issues." 2001-07-23. 2012-04-13. <http://www.globalissues.org/article/88/sierra-leone>.

Iweala, Uzodinma. "Slaughter of Innocence." The Guardian. 2007-05-25. 2012-07-26. <http://www.guardian.co.uk/books/2007/may/26/featuresreviews.guardianreview8>.

Boyd, William. "Babes in Arms." The New York Times Book Review 25 Feb. 2007: 12(L). Literature Resource Center. Web. 30 Oct. 2011.

Moorehead, Caroline. "Lost and found." Spectator 9 June 2007. Literature Resource Center. Web. 30 Oct. 2011

Quiz 1

1. **In what country did Beah live as a child?**
   A. Liberia
   B. Rhodesia
   C. Sierra Leone
   D. South Africa

2. **What was Ishmael Beah's home village as a child?**
   A. Kamator
   B. Mogbwemo
   C. Mattru Jong
   D. Kabati

3. **Where did Beah's grandmother live?**
   A. Kamator
   B. Mogbwemo
   C. Mattru Jong
   D. Kabati

4. **What kind of group do Beah and his childhood friends form?**
   A. a dance troupe
   B. a barbershop quartet
   C. a string quartet
   D. a rap group

5. **How old was Beah when the rebels attacked his village?**
   A. twelve
   B. fifteen
   C. ten
   D. six

6. **What sight convinces Beah that there is no returning home?**
   A. the mother with her dead baby
   B. the smoke rising from the west
   C. the desolation of Kabati
   D. the lunar eclipse

7. **What advice does the old man in Kabati offer to Beah?**
   A. to be like the moon and not complain
   B. to be like the snake and strike his enemies
   C. to seek his little brother back home
   D. to forget his family and move on

8. **Whose body does Beah dream he carries in a wheelbarrow?**
   A. his own
   B. Talloi's
   C. Gibrilla's
   D. his brother's

9. **What do the rebels call their practics of cutting off prisoner's fingers but leaving the thumbs intact?**
   A. "recruitment"
   B. "one love"
   C. "the hitchhiker"
   D. "surgery"

10. **What initials to the rebels carve into select prisoners' bodies?**
    A. RPG
    B. RUF
    C. SLR
    D. RJM

11. **What do the soldiers in Mattru Jong do when they learn of the rebels' approach?**
    A. evacuate the city
    B. draft young men into their ranks
    C. desert their posts
    D. dig trenches

12. **To where do the rebels drive the inhabitants of Mattru Jong?**
    A. the road
    B. the caves
    C. the river
    D. the forest

13. **After Beah and his friends attack the boy for two ears of corn, what do the boy's parents do?**
    A. attempt to poison them with bad water
    B. offer them all their food if they will only leave them alive
    C. call the local authorities to arrest the boys
    D. give each of the boys an ear of corn

14. **What is the highest age among the first rebels who capture Beah and his companions?**
    A. fifteen
    B. seventeen
    C. twenty-one
    D. thirty-two

15. **Why do the rebels patrol the forest around their captured village?**
    A. to find food so they can survive
    B. to locate escaped villagers who can give them information
    C. to find young men to recruit into the RUF
    D. to hunt for wild boar as trophies

16. **What do the rebels tell their chosen recruits they must do in order to be initiated into the RUF?**
    A. lead the attack on the next village
    B. carve the letters "RUF" into their flesh
    C. kill the weaker boys who were captured
    D. give them the names of their family and friends

17. **What problem do Beah and his friends have with traveling in a group of six?**
    A. the villagers are scared of large numbers of boys
    B. the number six is considered unlucky in Sierra Leone
    C. there is no clear winner in a vote
    D. they have six people to feed constantly

18. **Which of the boys is recognized by a traveller through an abandoned village?**
    A. Talloi
    B. Junior
    C. Gibrilla
    D. Khalilou

19. **What do the villagers of Kamator first ask the boys to do in exchange for food and shelter?**
   A. promise to marry their daughters
   B. plant cassava
   C. hunt wild boar
   D. stand guard

20. **When the threat of rebel attack seems unlikely, what do the villagers of Kamator put the boys to work doing?**
   A. farming
   B. fishing
   C. hunting
   D. building

21. **In what village does Beah last see Junior?**
   A. Kamator
   B. Mogbwemo
   C. Mattrru Jong
   D. Kabati

22. **How many days does Beah walk alone before encountering people?**
   A. six
   B. two
   C. nine
   D. eight

23. **Why is the family at the river afraid of Beah?**
   A. he has the initials "RUF" carved into his arm
   B. he does not speak the same language
   C. he is the same age as many RUF soldiers
   D. he steals food from them

24. **What did the village elder add to Beah's father's blessing on their home in Mogbwemo?**
   A. that the family would stay together in the spirit world
   B. that the family would stay true to the government
   C. that the family would have many children and grandchildren
   D. that the family would prosper and share their wealth

25. **What does the medicine Beah's grandfather put under his skin allow Beah to do?**
    A. swim like a fish
    B. resist disease
    C. control snakes
    D. blend in with the forest

Quiz 1 Answer Key

1. **(C)** Sierra Leone
2. **(B)** Mogbwemo
3. **(D)** Kabati
4. **(D)** a rap group
5. **(A)** twelve
6. **(A)** the mother with her dead baby
7. **(A)** to be like the moon and not complain
8. **(A)** his own
9. **(B)** "one love"
10. **(B)** RUF
11. **(C)** desert their posts
12. **(C)** the river
13. **(D)** give each of the boys an ear of corn
14. **(C)** twenty-one
15. **(C)** to find young men to recruit into the RUF
16. **(C)** kill the weaker boys who were captured
17. **(A)** the villagers are scared of large numbers of boys
18. **(C)** Gibrilla
19. **(D)** stand guard
20. **(A)** farming
21. **(A)** Kamator
22. **(A)** six
23. **(C)** he is the same age as many RUF soldiers
24. **(A)** that the family would stay together in the spirit world
25. **(C)** control snakes

Quiz 2

1. **What does Beah use in the place of soap when he bathes in the forest?**
   A. pea husks
   B. candle wax
   C. bark
   D. grass

2. **What does the medicine Beah's grandfather gives him to drink allow him to do?**
   A. go without water for weeks
   B. control snakes
   C. dance better than anyone else
   D. improve his memory

3. **What attacks Beah when he is alone in the forest?**
   A. a snake
   B. a panther
   C. wild pigs
   D. the rebels

4. **According to the story, how did the hunter trick the wild pigs?**
   A. he dropped down on them from trees
   B. he fed them meat which made them sleepy
   C. he wore a cloak which made him invisible
   D. he transformed himself into a pig

5. **When Beah encounters the other six boys in the forest, where are they headed?**
   A. Kamator
   B. Yele
   C. Mattru Jong
   D. Kabati

6. **What experience had Beah shared with three of the six boys he finds in the forest?**
   A. they had all lost an older brother
   B. they had all been in the same naming ceremony
   C. they had been flogged at school
   D. they all stood up to the rebels in Mattru Jong

7. **Why does the old man refuse to tell the seven boys his name?**
   A. he is afraid they will use it in witchcraft against him
   B. he is concerned they will tell others and have him arrested
   C. he does not remember his own name
   D. he wants to leave their minds room for other memories

8. **What situation makes the seven boys' encounters with other people more difficult?**
   A. the rumor that they are dangerous
   B. their RUF markings
   C. the fear that other people will turn them over to the rebels
   D. the fact that they carry a disease

9. **What is the source of the unfamiliar roaring noise the boys hear as they travel through the foreset?**
   A. an approaching storm
   B. the ocean
   C. a column of tanks
   D. an airplane

10. **What do the hostile fishermen take from Beah and his companions?**
   A. their weapons
   B. their food
   C. their music
   D. their shoes

11. **Why does the solitary fisherman refuse to tell the boys his name?**
   A. to keep them from using it in a magic ritual
   B. for their safety and his
   C. because he does not remember it
   D. he knows their families were enemies long ago

12. **What helps convince the chief of the fishing village that Beah and his companions are not rebels?**
   A. Beah's rap music tapes
   B. the arrival of Beah's family to the village
   C. Beah's familiar accent
   D. the fact that Saidu is the son of the previous chief

13. **What do the boys beleive the three white figures on the bridge to be?**
    A. angels
    B. rebels
    C. lepers
    D. ghosts

14. **What steals the boys' food as they sleep in an abandoned village?**
    A. another group of boys
    B. a wild dog
    C. a panther
    D. wild boars

15. **What do the hungry boys reluctantly eat in the forest?**
    A. rotten cassava
    B. kiwi fruit
    C. the dog they killed
    D. a fallen crow

16. **Who represents the family at Saidu's funeral?**
    A. Ishmael
    B. Masu
    C. Kanei
    D. Jumah

17. **What does Gasemu ask the boys to do before heading into the village?**
    A. carry bananas
    B. help him to walk
    C. wash their faces
    D. say a prayer

18. **What natural occurence saves the boys from the rebels who destroyed the refugee village?**
    A. an earthquake
    B. a lunar eclipse
    C. a tornado
    D. a rain storm

19. **Why does Ishmael hit Gasemu?**
   A. Gasemu attacks his friends
   B. Gasemu will not stop taunting him
   C. he believes Gasemu is a spy for the RUF
   D. he blames Gasemu for his not seeing his parents

20. **How do the boys find Yele?**
   A. one of them remembers the way
   B. they get directions from the locals
   C. they are taken there by soldiers
   D. they stumble upon it in the night

21. **Which village did Beah discover was occupied by government soldiers?**
   A. Mogwebo
   B. Yele
   C. Mattru Jong
   D. Nabari

22. **What is the first weapon Beah is given when he joins the military?**
   A. G3 Rifle
   B. RPG
   C. AK-47
   D. hand grenade

23. **What happens to Beah's rap tapes when he joins the military?**
   A. they are burned with his old clothes
   B. they are confiscated by older soldiers for their entertainment
   C. they are stolen by his tent-mates
   D. they are donated to the orphan relief movement

24. **What evidence does Lieutenant Jabati use to convince the villagers to remain and support the military?**
   A. a captured rebel spy who had lived with them for months
   B. capture rebel documents ordering a raid on the village
   C. the testimony of refugees from Mattru Jong
   D. the bodies of a man and young boy

25. **What injury kills Josiah?**
   - A. an infected leg muscle
   - B. a punctured lung
   - C. a head wound
   - D. a broken back

Quiz 2 Answer Key

1. **(D)** grass
2. **(D)** improve his memory
3. **(C)** wild pigs
4. **(D)** he transformed himself into a pig
5. **(B)** Yele
6. **(C)** they had been flogged at school
7. **(D)** he wants to leave their minds room for other memories
8. **(A)** the rumor that they are dangerous
9. **(B)** the ocean
10. **(D)** their shoes
11. **(B)** for their safety and his
12. **(A)** Beah's rap music tapes
13. **(D)** ghosts
14. **(B)** a wild dog
15. **(D)** a fallen crow
16. **(C)** Kanei
17. **(A)** carry bananas
18. **(D)** a rain storm
19. **(D)** he blames Gasemu for his not seeing his parents
20. **(C)** they are taken there by soldiers
21. **(B)** Yele
22. **(C)** AK-47
23. **(A)** they are burned with his old clothes
24. **(D)** the bodies of a man and young boy
25. **(D)** a broken back

Quiz 3

1. **Whose death spurs Beah to begin shooting the rebels?**
   A. Sheku's
   B. Josiah's
   C. Junior's
   D. Musa's

2. **What does Beah notice most of the dead rebels are wearing?**
   A. jewelry
   B. red shirts
   C. rebel flags
   D. sunglasses

3. **Where is Jumah stationed?**
   A. Mogbwemo
   B. Yele
   C. Mattru Jong
   D. Bauya

4. **Who chooses Beah to go with the UNICEF men?**
   A. Corporal Gadafi
   B. Beah himself
   C. Lieutenant Jabrati
   D. Alhaji

5. **What does Beah distainfully call the MPs?**
   A. "city soldiers"
   B. "dress-up dolls"
   C. "amateurs"
   D. "rich boys"

6. **Where do Beah, Alhaji, and Mambu secretly go?**
   A. Capetown
   B. Freetown
   C. Yele
   D. Mattru Jong

7. **What nickname does Lieutenant Jabrati give Beah?**
   A. King Cobra
   B. Black Mamba
   C. Green Snake
   D. Copperhead

8. **What nickname does Alhaji earn after his part in raiding a village for supplies?**
   A. Major Victory
   B. Death-Dealer
   C. Commando Boy
   D. Little Rambo

9. **What rank is Beah promoted to by Lieutenant Jabrati?**
   A. private first class
   B. corporal
   C. junior sergeant
   D. junior lieutenant

10. **What motivates the boys to attend their classes at the UNICEF compound?**
    A. the threat of harsh punshment for absence
    B. the offer of trips to Freetown
    C. the offer of pay for good grades
    D. the attractive female teachers

11. **What is the name of the nurse who befriends Beah?**
    A. Esther
    B. Rebekah
    C. Hagar
    D. Doris

12. **What gift does the nurse give to Beah?**
    A. a new pair of sneakers
    B. a walkman and rap tapes
    C. a notebook and pencils
    D. a sports jersey

13. **What statement does Beah grow frustrated at hearing the UNICEF workers repeat?**
    A. "We are your family now."
    B. "Your parents may still be alive."
    C. "It is not your fault."
    D. "You are still a child."

14. **How did Esther learn of Beah's interests?**
    A. hiring a private detective
    B. asking his friends
    C. from classroom questionnaires
    D. listening to him talk in his drug-induced sleep

15. **Who connects with Beah by discussing the history of Rastafarianism?**
    A. Leslie
    B. Esther
    C. Jumah
    D. Alhaji

16. **What is the name of Beah's long-lost uncle?**
    A. Mohamed
    B. Roger
    C. Tommy
    D. Gadafi

17. **What does Leslie call the act of reintegrating child soldiers into normal society?**
    A. "repatriation"
    B. "reconciliation"
    C. "resocialization"
    D. "relocation"

18. **How many biological children do Beah's uncle and aunt have?**
    A. five
    B. none
    C. four
    D. three

19. **Where does Allie take Beah to go dancing?**
   A. a gambling hall
   B. a pub
   C. a warehouse
   D. a street fair

20. **What does Mr. Kamara want Beah to interview to do?**
   A. address the United Nations
   B. rejoin the military as a ranking officer
   C. work as a manger for UNICEF
   D. become president of Sierra Leone

21. **What device mystifies Beah in the CAW building?**
   A. the telephone
   B. the television
   C. the water fountain
   D. the elevator

22. **Who is Beah's sponsor and chaperone to New York City?**
   A. Leslie
   B. Esther
   C. Dr. Tamba
   D. Uncle Tommy

23. **Who is the other boy who goes to New York with Beah?**
   A. Mohamed
   B. Bah
   C. Jumah
   D. Alhaji

24. **How does the immigration official in Freetown anger Beah?**
   A. he asks for proof that Beah was born in Sierra Leone
   B. he calls Beah "boy"
   C. he asks for a large bribe
   D. he says Beah reminds him of his dead son

25. **What is Uncle Tommy's reaction to the news that Beah will be going to New York?**
   A. he is angered and forbids it
   B. he cannot take it seriously
   C. he warns Beah about the violence of New York City
   D. he asks Beah to take the rest of the family

Quiz 3 Answer Key

1. **(D)** Musa's
2. **(A)** jewelry
3. **(D)** Bauya
4. **(C)** Lieutenant Jabrati
5. **(A)** "city soldiers"
6. **(B)** Freetown
7. **(C)** Green Snake
8. **(D)** Little Rambo
9. **(D)** junior lieutenant
10. **(B)** the offer of trips to Freetown
11. **(A)** Esther
12. **(B)** a walkman and rap tapes
13. **(C)** "It is not your fault."
14. **(C)** from classroom questionnaires
15. **(A)** Leslie
16. **(C)** Tommy
17. **(A)** "repatriation"
18. **(B)** none
19. **(B)** a pub
20. **(A)** address the United Nations
21. **(D)** the elevator
22. **(C)** Dr. Tamba
23. **(B)** Bah
24. **(A)** he asks for proof that Beah was born in Sierra Leone
25. **(B)** he cannot take it seriously

Quiz 4

1. **Where did Beah get his original views of New York City?**
    A. rap music
    B. internet
    C. television
    D. newspapers

2. **Who helps Beah prepare for his trip to New York?**
    A. Leslie
    B. Esther
    C. Dr. Tamba
    D. Mr. Kamara

3. **What new word does Beah learn upon arriving in New York City?**
    A. gangster
    B. car
    C. snow
    D. skyscraper

4. **How many children participated in the UN First Children's Parliament?**
    A. 12
    B. 57
    C. 99
    D. 150

5. **How many countries were represented at the UN First Childrens' Parliament?**
    A. 12
    B. 23
    C. 42
    D. 55

6. **During what time of year does Beah first arrive in New York?**
    A. spring
    B. winter
    C. summer
    D. fall

7. **What about Laura Simms helps Beah to connect with her instantly?**
   A. she is a storyteller
   B. she is also a child of war
   C. she likes rap music
   D. she knows Esther the nurse

8. **Who eventually adopts Beah?**
   A. Leslie
   B. Esther
   C. Dr. Tamba
   D. Laura Simms

9. **What amazing sight does Beah accidentally encounter in New York City?**
   A. the Statue of Liberty
   B. the Queensboro Bridge
   C. Times Square
   D. the Brooklyn Bridge

10. **What do Beah and Madoka find unusual about the train in New York?**
    A. the number of ads everywhere
    B. the graffiti is obscene
    C. everyone is quiet
    D. the low cost of transportation

11. **How old was Beah when he first addressed the UN?**
    A. 15
    B. 16
    C. 18
    D. 19

12. **What does Laura Simms give to Ishmael and Bah during the UN trip?**
    A. neckties
    B. coats and gloves
    C. computers
    D. eyeglasses

13. **Who declares himself the new president of Sierra Leone in 1997?**
    A. Charles Taylor
    B. Johnny Paul Koroma
    C. Tejan Kabbah
    D. Valentine Strasser

14. **What are the new AFRC/RUF soldiers called?**
    A. "Thanes"
    B. "Sobels"
    C. "Roofers"
    D. "Loyalists"

15. **On what day does Beah leave his uncle's home for good?**
    A. January 1
    B. October 31
    C. December 25
    D. July 4

16. **How does Uncle Tommy die?**
    A. teargas
    B. gunshot
    C. knife wound
    D. fever

17. **Where does Beah hide his money as he attempts to escape Sierra Leone?**
    A. his shoe
    B. his sock
    C. his jacket
    D. his backpack

18. **To what neighboring country does Beah escape from Sierra Leone?**
    A. Guinea
    B. Liberia
    C. Rhodesia
    D. South Africa

19. **What was the final destination of the refugee bus in Sierra Leone?**
    A. Freetown
    B. Mattru Jong
    C. Macaw
    D. Kambia

20. **What is the only language spoken in Guinea that Beah can understand?**
    A. English
    B. Mele
    C. Krio
    D. French

21. **In Pa Sesay's story, what does the monkey say will happen if the hunter shoots him?**
    A. the hunter's father will die
    B. the hunter's mother will die
    C. the monkey will grow more powerful
    D. the hunter will die

22. **In Pa Sesay's story, what does the monkey say will happen if the hunter does NOT shoot him?**
    A. the hunter's father will die
    B. the hunter's mother will die
    C. the hunter will live forever
    D. the monkey will grant him three wishes

23. **Why does Beah decide the hunter should shoot the monkey?**
    A. to ensure the survival of the monkey's rivals in nature
    B. because he knows the monkey is a liar
    C. because Beah does not love his mother
    D. to keep the monkey from putting other hunters in the same predicament

24. **Throughout the memoir, what provides a beautiful contrast to the violence occurring around Beah?**
    A. nature
    B. marriage ceremonies
    C. rap music
    D. childrens' games

25. **Where did Ishmael Beah go to college?**
   A. New York University
   B. Oberlin College
   C. Stanford
   D. Yale

Quiz 4 Answer Key

1. **(A)** rap music
2. **(D)** Mr. Kamara
3. **(C)** snow
4. **(B)** 57
5. **(B)** 23
6. **(B)** winter
7. **(A)** she is a storyteller
8. **(D)** Laura Simms
9. **(C)** Times Square
10. **(C)** everyone is quiet
11. **(A)** 15
12. **(B)** coats and gloves
13. **(B)** Johnny Paul Koroma
14. **(B)** "Sobels"
15. **(B)** October 31
16. **(D)** fever
17. **(B)** his sock
18. **(A)** Guinea
19. **(D)** Kambia
20. **(C)** Krio
21. **(B)** the hunter's mother will die
22. **(A)** the hunter's father will die
23. **(D)** to keep the monkey from putting other hunters in the same predicament
24. **(A)** nature
25. **(B)** Oberlin College

ClassicNotes

GradeSaver™

Getting you the grade since 1999™

ClassicNotes

GradeSaver™

Getting you the grade since 1999™

Made in the USA
Lexington, KY
07 February 2015